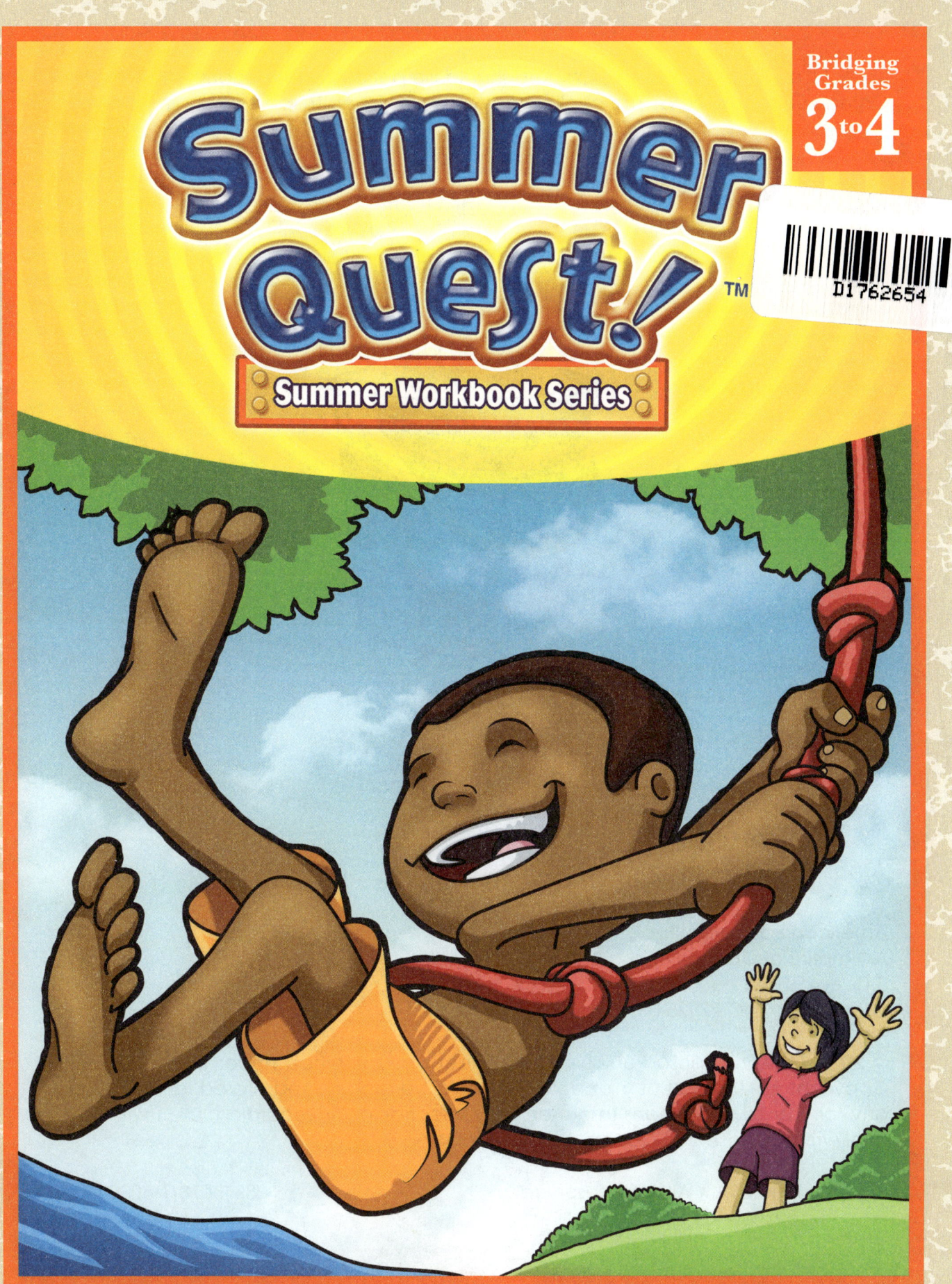

Note: All activities with young children should be performed with adult supervision. Caregivers should be aware of allergies, sensitivities, health, and safety issues.

American Education Publishing™
An imprint of Carson-Dellosa Publishing LLC
P.O. Box 35665
Greensboro, NC 27425 USA

© 2010, Carson-Dellosa Publishing LLC. Except as permitted under the United States Copyright Act, no part of this publication may be reproduced, stored, or distributed in any form or by any means (mechanically, electronically, recording, etc.) without the prior written consent of Carson-Dellosa Publishing LLC.

Printed in the USA • All rights reserved.　　　　　　　ISBN 978-1-62399-174-6

01-061137811

Table of Contents

Encouraging Summer Reading iv

Summer Reading List v

Skills Checklist vii

Summer Quest™ Activities 1–300

Blank Handwriting Page 301

Answer Key 302

Certificate of Completion 312

Stickers

Incentive Chart .... Inside Back Cover

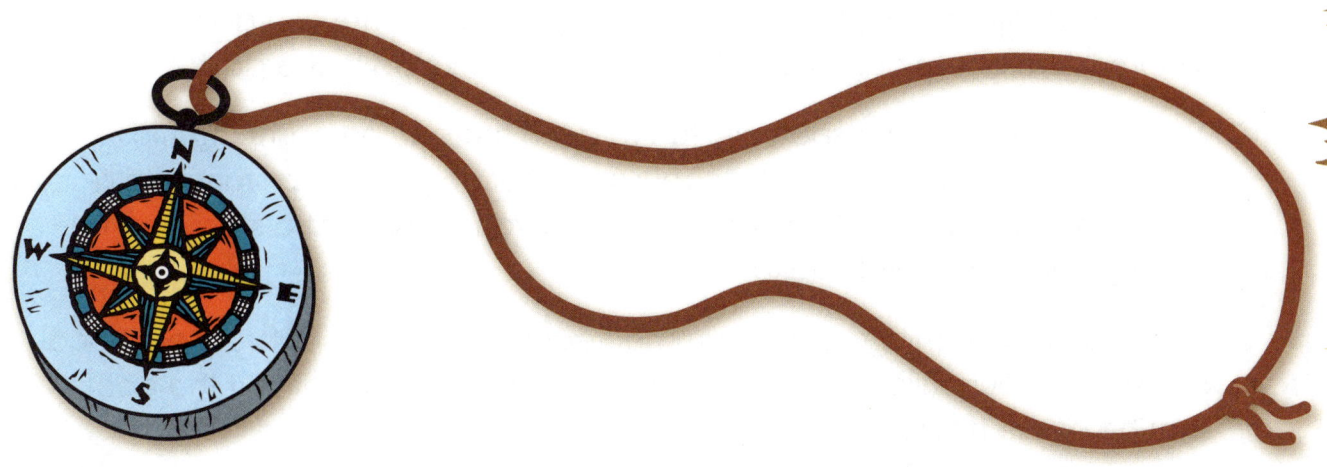

American Education Publishing™

Encouraging Summer Reading

Literacy is the single most important skill that your child needs to be successful in school. The following list includes ideas of ways that you can help your child discover the great adventures of reading!

- Establish a time for reading each day. Ask your child about what he or she is reading. Try to relate the material to an event that is happening this summer or to another book or story.

- Let your child see you reading for enjoyment. Talk about the great things that you discover when you read.

- Create a summer reading list. Choose books from the reading list (pages v–vi) or head to the library and explore the shelves. A general rule for selecting books at the appropriate reading level is to choose a page and ask your child to read it aloud. If he or she does not know more than five words on the page, the book may be too difficult.

- Read newspaper and magazine articles, recipes, menus, maps, and street signs on a daily basis to show your child the importance of reading.

- Find books that relate to your child's experiences. For example, if you are going camping, find a book about camping. This will help your child develop new interests.

- Visit the library each week. Let your child choose his or her own books, but do not hesitate to ask your librarian for suggestions. Often, librarians can recommend books based on what your child enjoyed in the past.

- Make up stories. This is especially fun to do in the car, on camping trips, or while waiting at the airport. Encourage your child to tell a story with a beginning, a middle, and an end. Or, have your child start a story and let other family members build on it.

- Encourage your child to join a summer reading club at the library or a local bookstore. Your child may enjoy talking to other children about the books that he or she has read.

Summer Reading List

The summer reading list includes fiction and nonfiction titles. Experts recommend that students entering the fourth grade read for at least 20 to 30 minutes each day. Ask your child questions about the story to reinforce comprehension.

Ackerman, Karen
The Night Crossing

Arnosky, Jim
Field Trips

Baylor, Byrd
The Table Where Rich People Sit

Bial, Raymond
A Handful of Dirt

Blume, Judy
Tales of a Fourth Grade Nothing

Catling, Patrick Skene
The Chocolate Touch

Cherry, Lynne
Flute's Journey: The Life of a Wood Thrush
A River Ran Wild

Cleary, Beverly
Beezus and Ramona
Ralph S. Mouse
Ramona Quimby, Age 8

Clifford, Eth
Flatfoot Fox and the Case of the Missing Schoolhouse

Dahl, Roald
Fantastic Mr. Fox
James and the Giant Peach

Danziger, Paula
Amber Brown Is Not a Crayon

DeJong, Meindert
The Wheel on the School

Donald, Rhonda Lucas
Endangered Animals

Dowell, Frances O'Roark
Phineas L. MacGuire...Erupts: The First Experiment

Eager, Edward
Half Magic

Frasier, Debra
Miss Alaineus: A Vocabulary Disaster

George, Jessica Day
Dragon Slippers

Graff, Lisa
The Thing About Georgie

Gregory, Kristiana
Across the Wide and Lonesome Prairie: The Oregon Trail Diary of Hattie Campbell, 1847

Summer Reading List (continued)

Griffin, Judith Berry
Phoebe the Spy

Hooper, Meredith
The Pebble in My Pocket: A History of Our Earth

Laden, Nina
Bad Dog

Lansky, Bruce (ed.)
The Best of Girls to the Rescue: Tales of Clever, Courageous Girls from Around the World

Lerner, Carol
Butterflies in the Garden

Lobel, Arnold
Fables

Locker, Thomas
Cloud Dance

Low, William
Old Penn Station

MacDonald, Betty
Mrs. Piggle-Wiggle

Murawski, Darlyne A.
Spiders and Their Webs

Pennypacker, Sara
Clementine

Pratt, Kristin Joy
A Walk in the Rainforest

Ringgold, Faith
Tar Beach

Rockwell, Anne
Why Are the Ice Caps Melting: The Dangers of Global Warming

Schotter, Roni
The Boy Who Loved Words

Seuss, Dr.
Oh, the Places You'll Go!

Spyri, Johanna
Heidi

St. George, Judith
So You Want to Be President?

Steig, William
Dominic

Van Allsburg, Chris
The Garden of Abdul Gasazi

Waters, Kate
Samuel Eaton's Day: A Day in the Life of a Pilgrim Boy
Sarah Morton's Day: A Day in the Life of a Pilgrim Girl

Skills Checklist

With this book, your child will have the opportunity to practice and acquire many new skills. Keep track of the skills you practice together. Put a check beside each skill your child completes.

Math

- [ ] addition
- [ ] division
- [ ] fact families
- [ ] fractions
- [ ] geometry
- [ ] graphs and grids
- [ ] measurement
- [ ] multiplication
- [ ] number ordering
- [ ] patterns
- [ ] place value
- [ ] probability
- [ ] rounding
- [ ] statistics
- [ ] story problems
- [ ] subtraction
- [ ] symmetry
- [ ] time and money

Language Arts

- [ ] dictionary and reference skills
- [ ] grammar
- [ ] following directions
- [ ] handwriting
- [ ] parts of speech
- [ ] phonics
- [ ] punctuation
- [ ] puzzles and riddles
- [ ] reading informational text
- [ ] reading stories
- [ ] sentence structure
- [ ] spelling
- [ ] vocabulary
- [ ] word parts
- [ ] writing
- [ ] writing poetry

Skills Checklist (continued)

Physical Fitness/Health

- [x] fitness activities
- [ ] movement
- [ ] outdoor activities
- [x] running
- [ ] stretching

Social Studies

- [ ] character development
- [ ] geography
- [x] history
- [ ] map skills

Science

- [ ] experiment

▶ Solve each problem.   June 10th Tuseday — To Ballet

1. The answers to addition problems are called ___sums___.

2. The answers to subtraction problems are called ___differece___.

3. 44 − 34 = __3__
4. 25 + 23 = __10__
5. 40 + 29 = __14__
6. 50 − 15 = __48__
7. 40 − 38 = __5__
8. 12 + 15 = __69__
9. 29 − 13 = __6__
10. 23 + 23 = __37__
11. 38 + 20 = __35__
12. 17 − 5 = __2__
13. 13 + 16 = __8__
14. 26 + 43 = __27__
15. 19 − 8 = __9__
16. 39 − 27 = __16__
17. 42 + 14 = __10__
18. 28 − 5 = __46__
19. 26 + 13 = __11__
20. 51 + 27 = __58__

Go for an animal observation walk around your neighborhood. Take a pencil and notebook with you. Write down the different animals you see. Use tally marks for multiple viewings of the same kind of animal.

American Education Publishing™

▶ **Trace the letters in cursive.**

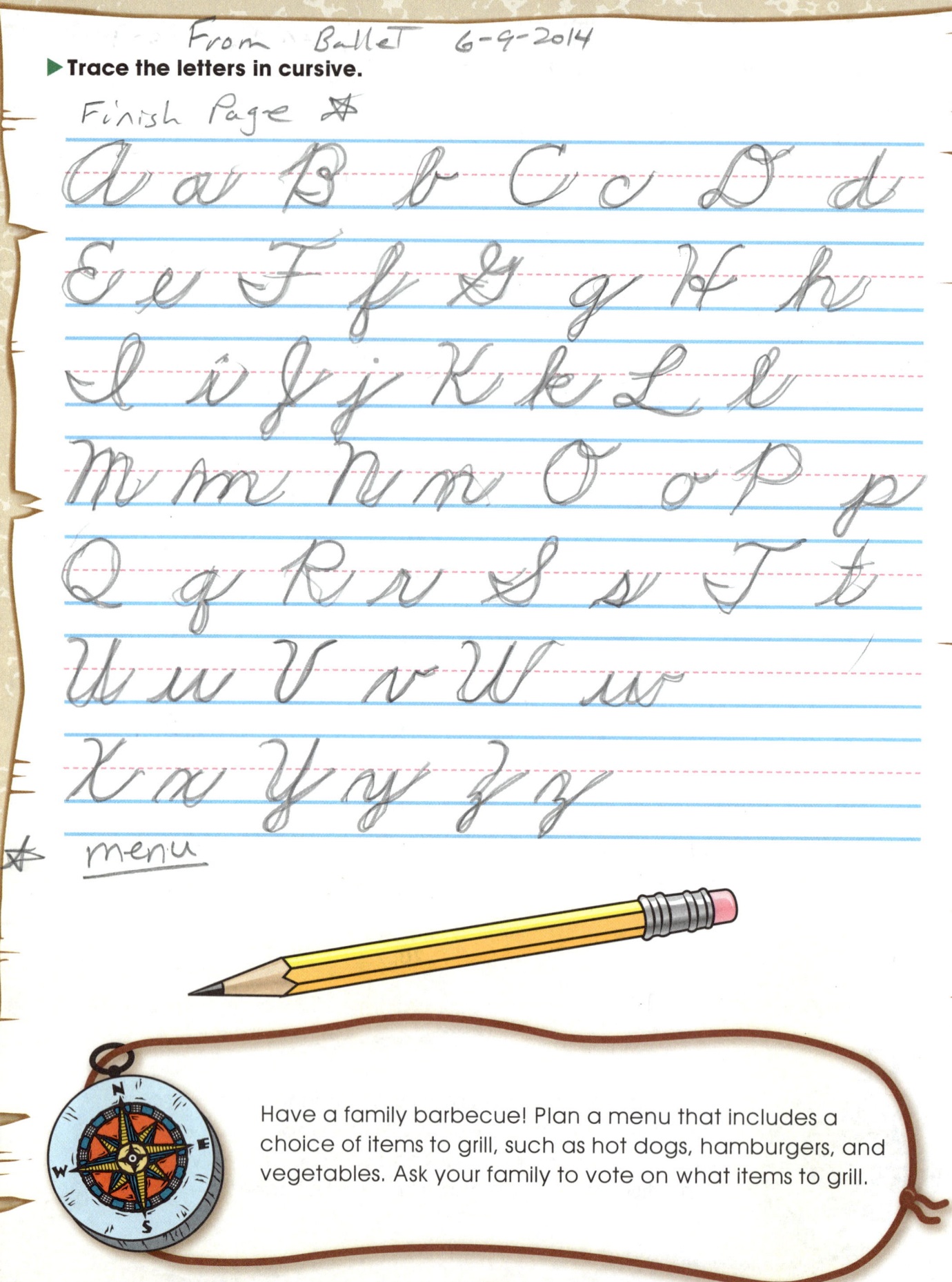

Have a family barbecue! Plan a menu that includes a choice of items to grill, such as hot dogs, hamburgers, and vegetables. Ask your family to vote on what items to grill.

▶ **Read the passage. Then, answer the questions.**

Glaciers

A glacier is a large, thick mass of ice. It forms when snow hardens into ice over a long period of time. It might not look like it, but glaciers can move. Glaciers usually move slowly. If a lot of ice melts at once, a glacier may surge forward, or move suddenly. Most glaciers are found in Antarctica (the continent at the South Pole) or in Greenland (a country near the North Pole). Areas with glaciers receive a lot of snowfall in the winter and have cool summers. Most glaciers are located in the mountains, where few people live. Occasionally, glaciers can cause flooding in cities and towns. Falling ice from glaciers may block the path of people hiking on trails farther down the mountain. Icebergs are large, floating pieces of ice that have broken off from glaciers. Icebergs can cause problems for ships at sea.

1. What is the main idea of this passage?
    A. Icebergs can be dangerous to ships.
    B. Glaciers are large masses of ice found mainly in the mountains.
    C. People usually live far away from glaciers.

2. How does a glacier form? *When snow hardens into ice over a long period of time*

3. Where are most glaciers located? *Antarctica or greenland greenland*

4. What is the weather like where glaciers are found? *There is a lot of snowfall in winter and cool summers*

Go outside with an adult family member on a clear night. Look at the incredible sights in the night sky. What do you notice about the moon? Talk about what you observe.

From Nehas

▶ **Homophones** are words that sound the same but have different meanings and are spelled differently. Write the correct homophone from the parentheses to complete each sentence.

1. I have ___two___ more days of school. (to, (two))

2. Have you ___read___ this book before? ((read), red)

3. That lion has large ___paws___ . ((paws), pause)

4. I like that song ___too___ . (two, (too))

5. The boys had ___to___ much work to do before dark. (too, to)

6. ___Red___ is my favorite color. (Red, Read)

7. We are going ___to___ Lake Louise this summer. (to, two)

8. Please ___pause___ the movie for a minute. (paws, pause)

Help save Earth's resources. Next time you go shopping, bring your own paper, cloth, or plastic bag with you.

4

American Education Publishing™

▶ **Follow the directions.**

1. Draw a square around the greatest number.
2. Count by 2s to 40. Underline the numbers you use.
3. Draw a triangle around the number that is 4 less than 62.
4. Draw an X over each odd number.
5. Circle all of the uppercase letters. Write the letters you circled in order, starting with the top row and moving left to right.

_____

b	r	q	e	o	S	c	r	y	10	6	8
U	y	10	6	2	4	M	z	l	q	a	i
6	v	0	7	8	M	p	2	10	17	12	l
r	b	14	18	b	e	16	f	h	19	E	s
18	5	14	7	2	p	m	n	z	58	20	s
94	86	22	2	R	17	I	0	24	n	x	c
26	39	3	a	d	e	28	g	S	52	19	30
7	j	F	k	32	y	34	4	31	t	10	36
0	n	e	n	38	o	80	98	U	47	x	p
w	m	m	11	N	3	14	39	c	r	e	t
q	u	v	9	7	6	w	5	40	w	13	19

Look at your room. Note all the items in your room, such as your bed, a bookshelf, a desk, and the trash can. Take a pencil and paper and draw a map of your room.

American Education Publishing™

▶ Use the fact family in each circle to make number sentences.

1.

$8 + 7 = 15$
$7 + 8 = 15$
$15 - 8 = 7$
$15 - 7 = 8$

2.

$8 + 9 = 15$
$9 + 8 = 15$
$15 - 8 = 9$
$15 - 9 = 8$

3.

$8 + 6 = 14$
$6 + 8 = 14$
$14 - 8 = 6$
$14 - 6 = 8$

Your best friend is going to a great summer camp. You would like to go too. Make a list of three ways you could raise money to attend the camp.

▶ **Trace the letters in cursive.**

a a a a a a c c c c c

e e e e e e m m m m

m m n n o o o o o o

s s s s s r r r r r

v v v v v x x x x x x

w w w w w w w w w w

l l l l l l t t t t t t t

b b b b b b b b b b b

Toward the end of the day, make a three-panel comic strip. Draw what you did in the morning, afternoon, and evening. Post your comic strip for family members to see.

▶ Add to find each sum.

1. 634 + 268 = 902
2. 987 + 489 = 1,476
3. 493 + 277 = 770
4. 888 + 245 = 1,133
5. 732 + 299 = 1,031
6. 947 + 276 = 1,223
7. 496 + 394 = 890
8. 557 + 323 = 880
9. 347 + 254 = 621
10. 743 + 458 = 1,201
11. 296 + 109 = 405
12. 636 + 587 = 1,223

The best summer desserts can be fresh fruits that are in season. Find out what fresh fruits are in season where you live. Enjoy one of these fresh fruits with your family.

▶ Identify each sentence type. Write **D** for declarative, **IN** for interrogative, **E** for exclamatory, or **IM** for imperative.

1. __D__ Whales have to eat a lot of food.
2. __IN__ Why do you think that?
3. __D__ Whales are the largest animals living today.
4. __D__ Blue whales can weigh up to 200 tons each.
5. __E__ They are gigantic!
6. __E__ That is unbelievable!
7. __IM__ Find out how much other animals eat.
8. __IN__ How much do lions eat?
9. __D__ They eat 50 or 60 pounds of meat daily.
10. __E__ A lion can eat that much in one meal!

Be a weather reporter! Check the weather forecast for the day and present the forecast to your family members.

American Education Publishing™

▶ **Read the story. Then, write the correct prefix in each blank. Use dis-, in-, re-, or un-.**

Unsolved Mystery

My Uncle Paul worked in a bookstore. Uncle Paul always helped me find books to read. He was never (1.) __dis__ pleased if I asked him for help.

I (2.) __re__ call the day I asked for a book about unsolved mysteries. Uncle Paul (3.) __dis__ covered some on the very top of the back shelf. They were dirty and smelled dusty. They looked as if they had been (4.) __un__ touched for years. I started to read one. As I looked (5.) __in__ side, I noticed that some of the pages were missing from the very end of the book. "Oh no!" I said. "This story is (6.) __in__ complete. Now, I'll never know how it ends." I must have looked pretty (7.) __dis__ appointed because Uncle Paul tried to cheer me up. He said, "I don't mean to be (8.) __un__ kind, but you wanted to read about unsolved mysteries. I think you (9.) __dis__ covered a real unsolved mystery!"

Write a note to a family member wishing him a good day. Place the note where it will be easily discovered.

▶ Read the paragraph. Then, write *fiction* or *nonfiction* on the line. In the space provided, draw a picture of what a forest might look like after a group of army ants traveled through.

Army Ants

Army ants are one of the most feared types of ants. These ants are very destructive and can eat all living things in their paths. Army ants travel at night in groups of hundreds of thousands through the tropical forests of Africa and South America.

1. nonfiction

Stand with paper and pencil at your front door. Count the number of steps to your bedroom. Write it down. Next, count the number of steps from your bedroom to the kitchen. Write it down and add the two numbers together. What is the total number of steps you have taken?

▶ **Solve each word problem.**

1. I read 6 books in June. I read 3 books in July. I read 7 books in August. How many books did I read these three months?

    +6
    +7
    +3
    ---
    16 = sixteen books.

2. Carla went on a weekend trip. She took 16 photos. She printed only 8 photos. How many photos did she not print?

    16
    − 8
    ---
    9 = nine photos.

3. I saw 12 birds on Monday. I saw 8 birds on Tuesday. I saw 7 birds on Wednesday. How many birds did I see in all?

    12
    + 8
    + 7
    ---
    27 = twenty seven birds

4. Sue counted 14 fish and 9 tadpoles in the pond. How many fewer tadpoles were there than fish?

    14
    − 9
    ---
    7 = seven tadpoles

With an adult family member, boil several eggs. After the eggs have cooled, use markers to draw a funny face on each egg. Now you are ready to serve smiles for breakfast!

▶ Read each group of words. Write **S** if it is a sentence or **F** if it is a fragment.

1. __S__ Chris slid into home plate.

2. __F__ In the top row I.

3. __F__ Watched a squirrel.

4. __S__ The clown's funny hat fell off.

5. __F__ Pulled a wagon down.

6. __S__ In the forest, we saw three deer.

7. __S__ A plane landed at the airport.

8. __F__ Our team started to.

9. __S__ Mom broke a window when she was young.

With a family member, walk around your home and look for pictures of the people in your family. What do you notice? Talk about what you observe in each picture. Did you learn anything new about your family?

▶ **Look at the key and the example for a three-digit number. Then, fill in the missing information below.**

KEY:
O = hundreds
/ = tens
• = ones

EXAMPLE:
Standard number: 482
Expanded notation: 400 + 80 + 2
Pictorial model: OOOO //////// ••

1. Standard number: 327
   Expanded notation: 300 + 20 + 7
   Pictorial model: OOO // •••••••

2. Standard number: 254
   Expanded notation: 200 + 50 + 4
   Pictorial model: OO ///// ••••

3. Standard number: 845
   Expanded notation: 800 + 40 + 5
   Pictorial model: OOOOOOOO //// •••••

Did you know that six-pack rings can hurt animals? Prevent this by cutting your six-pack rings into small pieces before throwing them in the garbage. This is a simple way you can help make the environment a safer place!

▶ An **adjective** is a word that describes a noun. Circle the adjective that describes each underlined noun.

1. Some prairie dogs live in (large) communities under the ground.

2. A mother prairie dog makes a nest of (dried) plants in the spring.

3. She gives birth to a litter of (four) pups.

4. She is a (good) mother and takes care of her pups.

5. The pups are ready to venture outside after (six) weeks.

6. The pups have (many) friends.

Food, food, food! With a family member, go to your kitchen and locate the various places where food is stored. What do you notice? Talk about the food storage patterns you observe in the kitchen cupboards and in the refrigerator.

▶ Read each title below. Write **F** on the line if you believe the story is *fiction*, **NF** if you think it is *nonfiction*, or **B** if you think it is a *biography*.

Fiction:	a story that is made up or is not factual
Nonfiction:	a true or factual story
Biography:	a story about a real person's life

__F__ 1. Kelly's Rainbow Zebra

__B__ 2. The Life of Albert Einstein

__NF__ 3. How Cars Are Made

__F__ 4. My Trip to Mars

__F__ 5. We Rode on a Unicorn

__B__ 6. All about Susan B. Anthony

__NF__ 7. Plants of North America

__NF__ 8. The Battles of the Civil War

How do you help out at home? Write a list of five ways you help your family. Then, make a five-panel comic strip showing yourself helping at home. Post your comic strip for family members to see, letting them know your key roles!

▶ **Write each number.**

EXAMPLE:

6 tens
8 ones

___68___

1. 9 tens
   4 ones

   ___94___

2. 5 tens
   0 ones

   ___50___

3. 10 tens
   0 ones

   ___100___

4. 6 tens
   3 hundreds
   8 ones

   ___368___

5. 4 hundreds
   0 tens
   2 ones

   ___402___

6. 5 ones
   6 hundreds
   7 tens

   ___675___

7. 9 hundreds
   3 ones
   5 tens

   ___953___

8. 3 hundreds
   7 ones
   2 tens

   ___327___

Be a home inspector. Take a pencil and paper and walk around your home, making tally marks for the number of windows in each room. After your window inspection, count the tally marks. How many windows are there altogether? Which room has the most windows?

▶ **Read the passage. Then, answer the questions.**

The Olympic Games

During the Olympic Games, people from all over the world gather to compete in different sporting events. The original Olympics were held in Greece around 776 BC. Athletes came together every four years to run races of different lengths. Those who won were given wreaths of olive branches. The modern Olympics were first held in 1896 in Greece. In 1994, the International Olympic Committee decided that the summer and winter Olympic Games should be held in different years. This means that every two years, thousands of people representing more than 200 countries come together to compete in either summer or winter sports. Today's top athletes receive gold, silver, or bronze medals and compete in hundreds of different events. The Olympics give each host country a chance to show its culture both to the people who come there and to the people who watch on TV. The sports may be different than in the original Olympics, but the spirit of goodwill and good sportsmanship is still the same.

1. What is the main idea of this passage?
    A. The Olympics are held every four years.
    B. People come to the Olympics from all over the world to compete in different sports.
    C. Today's top athletes receive gold, silver, or bronze medals.

2. How do the Olympics help people learn about different cultures? _____

   To host country a chance to show it's culture both to the people who come there and to the people who watch TV.

Be a news reporter! Your assignment is to survey pet owners about why people have pets. Talk with pet owners in your neighborhood as well as with your friends about their reasons for having pets. Share your report with your family members.

▶ **Add to find each sum.**

1. 24
   41
   + 32

   97

2. 91
   28
   + 13

   132

3. 35
   66
   + 37

   138

4. 22
   61
   + 84

   167

5. 16
   10
   + 31

   57

6. 45
   32
   + 48

   125

7. 45
   52
   + 21

   118

8. 28
   39
   + 21

   88

9. 27
   65
   + 85

   177

Open your refrigerator door and look inside. Observe the shelves and freezer. Note the items you see and their specific locations. Use a pencil and paper to make a map of your refrigerator. Post your refrigerator map to assist family members.

▶ Write the correct forms of each adjective.

	Adjectives That Compare Two Nouns	Adjectives That Compare More Than Two Nouns
EXAMPLE: long	*longer*	*longest*
1. soft	softer	softest
2. large	larger	largest
3. flat	flater	flatest
4. sweet	sweeter	sweetest
5. wide	wider	widest
6. cool	cooler	coolest

Get ready to help a neighbor take a group of five-year-olds to the zoo! The neighbor has asked you to make a list of safety rules promoting car and zoo safety. Make a poster showing the rules so that the young children will clearly understand them.

▶ **Add to find each sum.**

1. 3.76
  + 2.66

  6.42

2. 3.49
  + 2.33

  5.82

3. 8.78
  + 2.87

  11.65

4. 4.36
  + 2.96

  7.32

5. 9.48
  + 3.48

  12.96

6. 4.98
  + 4.39

  9.37

7. 4.77
  + 2.98

  7.75

8. 3.96
  + 4.74

  8.70

9. 9.01
  + 1.09

  10.08

10. 5.72
  + 3.69

  9.41

11. 7.14
  + 6.94

  13.08

12. 6.57
  + 3.28

  9.85

Create the dinner menu for Saturday evening. Look through magazines for pictures of foods you would like to include on the menu. Cut out the pictures and glue them on a piece of construction paper. Share your menu with family members. How do they feel about your menu?

▶ Use the line in front of each noun to write an adjective that describes the noun.

1. __soft__ rain
2. __glass__ table
3. __fake__ flower
4. __Thundersormy__ day
5. __roden__ fruit
6. __flower__ petal
7. __tall__ grass
8. __Best__ friend
9. __long__ lake
10. __hugemungus__ house

When you open the refrigerator, the cold air you feel coming out is trading places with warm air going in. This means the refrigerator has to use extra electricity to cool back down. Post a blank piece of paper on the refrigerator door. Ask family members to make a tally mark each time they open the refrigerator door. At the end of the day, count the tally marks. Share the results with family members.

American Education Publishing™

▶ **Follow the directions below to learn how to increase your flexibility.**

There are a lot of benefits to stretching. Do you like basketball, dancing, or another physical activity that requires you to move, run, or jump? If so, then you should try to improve your flexibility. Whatever your favorite physical activity is, set a goal for yourself to complete at least one stretch every day that will help make you a better athlete. For example, if you like tennis and want to improve your backhand, practice a trunk-twist stretch at least twice a day. As with all stretching exercises, start slowly. Gradually increase your stretching as you become more flexible. This is how professional athletes improve their abilities. So, stretch for better performance!

Tell your family members that you will pick up the mail. Make a two-column chart, labeling one column "Family Member" and the other column "Number of Items." Count the number of items in the mail for each family member and fill out the chart. How many items were delivered to your home? Who got the most mail? Share the results with your family.

▶ Write different ways to make the amount of money in each problem. Use real money to help you.

EXAMPLE:

10¢
- 10 pennies
- 2 nickels
- 1 nickel, 5 pennies
- 1 dime

1. $1.00
- 100 pennies
- 19 nickels
- 10 dimes
- 5 dimes and 75 nickles

2. 25¢
- 1 quarter
- 2 dimes and 1 nickle
- 25 pennies
- 5 nickles

3. $1.60
- 1 dolar bill and 6 dimes
- 160 pennies
- 16 dimes

Are you going somewhere with your family? Perhaps you are going over to a relative's home or to the grocery store. Encourage your family to think twice before you go in a car. Talk with your family about possible alternatives to driving the car. Is where you are going close enough to walk? Can you take a bus or train?

▶ Write an adjective in each blank to complete each sentence.

1. A __friendly__ family moved in next door yesterday.

2. The bear has __soft__, __brown__ fur.

3. The __gorgeous__ birds woke me up this morning. *pretty*

4. Her __rainbow__ balloon floated away.

▶ **Demonstrative pronouns** identify specific nouns. Write the correct demonstrative pronoun (*this*, *that*, *these*, or *those*) to complete each sentence. Use *this* and *that* with singular nouns. Use *these* and *those* with plural nouns.

5. __This__ book is one of my favorites.

6. Is __this__ hat the one Mom wanted?

7. __That__ planet is very far away.

8. __Those__ ducks didn't come back to the pond this year.

Your shadow changes throughout the day. Take a tape measure outside three times during the day. Each time, have a partner measure your shadow and write down the measurements. How does your shadow change throughout the day?

▶ **Write each number.**

1. five hundred sixty-one 561
2. eight hundred 800
3. four hundred eighty-six 486
4. one hundred fifty 150

▶ **Count how many are in each set. Write each number.**

5.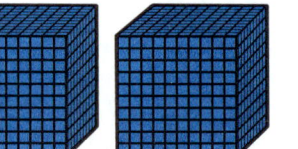

   2021

6.

   4,011

Take a pen and a notebook outside and find a place to sit. Look around and observe the various things you see. Make a list of 20 things you see. Can you expand the list to 30? To 40?

▶ A **compound word** is made of two words that have been put together to make a new word. Use the words from the word bank to make a compound word that matches each description.

~~bath~~	storm	back	mates
apple	horse	~~tub~~	pine
team	snow	scare	crow

EXAMPLE:

a place where you can go to get clean

bathtub

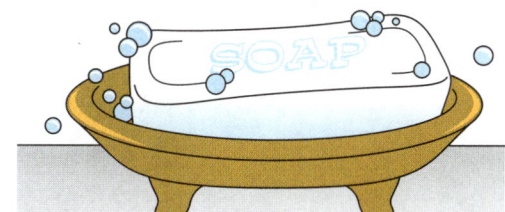

1. a fruit with spiky skin

   _____

2. what farmers put in cornfields to scare birds away

   _____

3. a type of weather event that some places get in the winter

   _____

4. if you ride on a horse, you have this kind of ride

   _____

5. people who play on a team with you

   _____

You are the lifeguard at the local swimming pool. You want to make certain that all the swimmers respect you. Create a 30-second commercial promoting respect for the lifeguard. Share your commercial with friends and family members.

▶ **Round each number to the nearest 10.**

EXAMPLE:

28 = _30_

1. 85 = _____

2. 13 = _10_

3. 44 = _____

4. 33 = _30_

5. 92 = _____

6. 78 = _80_

7. 18 = _____

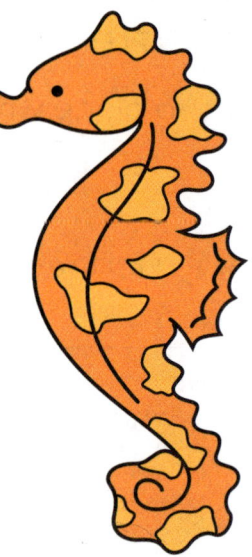

▶ **Round each number to the nearest 100.**

8. 767 = _800_

9. 211 = _____

10. 841 = _800_

11. 587 = _____

You just received a neighborhood good citizen award. Make a list of five things you might have done to receive this award. Review your list with a family member. Talk about the different items on your list. Which of the ideas might you actually do?

28

▶ **Common nouns** name any one of a group of things. **Proper nouns** name a specific person, place, or thing. Each sentence has one common noun and one proper noun. Write the common noun to the left of the sentence and the proper noun to the right.

Common Nouns　　　　　　　　　　　　　　　　**Proper Nouns**

cousin　　　1. My cousin lives in Spain.　　　Spain

bear　　　　2. Smokey is a famous bear.　　　Smokey

family　　　3. My family ate at Pizza Barn.　　Pizza Barn

city　　　　4. Ogden is a beautiful city.　　　Ogden

_____　5. Isaac Newton was a scientist.　_____

_____　6. The first satellite was Sputnik I.　_____

_____　7. George Eastman made cameras.　_____

_____　8. The Pilgrims sailed for two months.　_____

Your job is to promote a water-saving campaign at home. The campaign is called Presto, On! Presto, Off! Note places where family members might need reminders to turn off the faucet. At these places, make Presto, On! Presto, Off! signs. Let your family know that the signs are there to encourage them to conserve water.

▶ **Rewrite the paragraph with the correct punctuation and capitalization.**

last summer we went camping in colorado we went hiking and swimming every day one time i actually saw a baby white-tailed deer with spots we also took photos of a lot of pretty rocks flowers and leaves we had a great time i didn't want to leave

You are a famous chef known for creating delicious sandwiches. Create a new sandwich. Use a pencil and paper to list the particular ingredients in the sandwich. Be sure to give the sandwich a special name.

▶ **Add to find each sum.**

1.
   ¹
   57
   42
   + 33
   ___
   132

2.
   ¹
   38
   46
   + 23
   ___
   107

3.
   ¹
   17
   36
   + 22
   ___
   75

4.
   ¹
   85
   36
   + 74
   ___
   195

5.
   ¹
   76
   23
   + 67
   ___
   166

6.
   56
   21
   + 32
   ___
   109

7.
   ²
   39
   48
   + 59
   ___
   146

8.
   ¹
   45
   23
   + 54
   ___
   122

9.
   24
   51
   + 76

10.
   25
   45
   + 56

11.
   55
   21
   + 37

12.
   33
   30
   + 36

Report on the transportation in your neighborhood. Take a pencil and notebook and go for a walk around your neighborhood. Write the different forms of transportation you see. Use tally marks for multiple viewings of the same kind of transportation. What form of transportation do you see most often? Least often?

▶ **Negative words** usually have *no* in them. Avoid using two negative words in the same sentence. Underline the second negative word in each sentence. Then, write a positive word to replace the word you underlined.

Negative	Positive	Negative	Positive
no, none	a, any, one	no one	anyone, someone
nothing	anything, something	nobody	anybody, somebody
nowhere	anywhere, somewhere	never	ever

1. There are no flamingos living nowhere near me. _____

2. Can't nobody tell me where they live? _____

3. There are not no other wading birds as big and colorful. _____

4. I will not never forget the day that I saw my first flamingo. _____

5. There must not be nothing else like flamingos. _____

Make a list of 10 things you could do to help at home, such as take out the trash, wash the dishes, or clean your room. Decide on one thing to do and then do it today.

▶ **Rewrite the numbers in each row in order from least to greatest.**

1. 6,283   683   561   656   _____ _____ _____ _____

2. 8,899   882   8,311   411   _____ _____ _____ _____

3. 6,420   742   642   7,420   _____ _____ _____ _____

4. 4,444   444   4,000   4,040   _____ _____ _____ _____

▶ **Rewrite the numbers in each row in order from greatest to least.**

5. 737   3,778   7,138   397   _____ _____ _____ _____

6. 998   899   9,989   9,998   _____ _____ _____ _____

7. 242   786   472   6,487   _____ _____ _____ _____

8. 565   6,565   5,565   665   _____ _____ _____ _____

Go outside with your family on a clear night. Look at the amazing nighttime sky. What do you notice about the stars? Draw a picture to show what you observe.

▶ A noun names a person, a place, or a thing. An action verb tells what a noun is doing. Circle the nouns. Underline the verbs.

elephant	sang	ate	fixed
laugh	tent	Mr. Chip	team
book	California	guitar	landed
Lake Street	cleaned	yell	played
visited	Kent	write	strength
engine	jump	broccoli	leap

Help your family save Earth's resources! Make sure that there is a cloth towel by the sink. Encourage your family members to grab the cloth towel instead of a paper towel each time they wash their hands.

▶ **Circle the word in each row that is divided correctly into syllables.**

1. cact/us   ca/ctus   cac/tus   c/actus

2. bli/ster   blist/er   blis/ter   bl/ister

3. al/ways   a/lways   alw/ays   alwa/ys

4. har/bor   ha/rbor   harb/or   harbo/r

5. fl/ower   flo/wer   flowe/r   flow/er

6. bas/ket   bask/et   ba/sket   baske/t

7. obe/ys   o/beys   ob/eys   obey/s

Become a closet organizer. Use a pencil and paper to make a list of all the things you see in your closet. Then, create a plan of action for organizing the various items. Now, start organizing!

▶ **Study the examples below. Then, compare each set of numbers. Write < (less than), > (greater than), or = (equal to) on each line.**

EXAMPLES:

375 < 6,200   7,000 = 7,000   3,482 > 2,843

1. 620 ____ 6,200
2. 9,286 ____ 13,489
3. 45,015 ____ 45,016
4. 493 ____ 439
5. 724 ____ 724
6. 397,124 ____ 387,425
7. 6,432 ____ 16,408
8. 3,080 ____ 3,800

Convince your adult family members to let you go on a vacation with your friend's family. Make a list of at least three reasons that you should be permitted to go. Are your reasons convincing enough?

▶ **Syllables** represent the number of vowel sounds heard in words.

> **EXAMPLES**:
> **what** – 1 vowel sound and 1 syllable
> **pencil** – 2 vowel sounds and 2 syllables
> **animal** – 3 vowel sounds and 3 syllables

▶ Read each word below. Use the line to write the number of syllables in the word. Listen to make sure that the number of vowel sounds equals the number of syllables for each word.

1. apple _____
2. prune _____
3. cherry _____
4. banana _____
5. lemon _____
6. pear _____
7. watermelon _____
8. plum _____

At the end of the day, make a three-panel comic strip showing what you would like to do the next day. Post your comic strip so family members can see your plans.

▶ **Compare each set of numbers. Write < (less than) or > (greater than) on each line.**

1. 126 _____ 261
2. 999 _____ 899
3. 126 _____ 226
4. 342 _____ 231
5. 524 _____ 624
6. 832 _____ 932
7. 619 _____ 719
8. 267 _____ 367
9. 580 _____ 579
10. 1,638 _____ 738
11. 4,206 _____ 5,206
12. 3,487 _____ 3,748

Summertime gives you extra time to read for fun and enjoyment. Organize a book swap. Pick a day and then invite your friends to participate with you in trading old books.

▶ **Synonyms** are words that mean about the same thing. Complete each sentence with a word from the word bank that is a synonym for the underlined word.

| silent | lid | small | tug |
| tip | mistake | happy | tear |

1. Dan's pencil point was dull, so he had to sharpen the _____ .

2. The top came off of the ant farm, but I quickly replaced the _____ .

3. The cheerful girl was very _____ when she got an A on her science project.

4. Anna got a rip in her jeans, so her mother repaired the _____ .

5. Gina had to pull and _____ the heavy chair to move it.

6. Dana was quiet because her mother asked her to be _____ while the baby slept.

7. I made an error, and the teacher showed me my _____ .

8. The tiny earring was hard to find because it was so _____ .

Be the weather reporter for your family. Check the weather forecast for the day and place signs around your home that indicate the weather for the day.

▶ **Write the abbreviation for each word.**

EXAMPLE:

December ___*Dec.*___   1. Wednesday _____

2. January _____   3. August _____

4. Sunday _____   5. Thursday _____

6. February _____   7. September _____

8. Monday _____   9. Friday _____

10. March _____   11. October _____

12. Tuesday _____   13. Saturday _____

14. April _____   15. November _____

At the end of the day, write a note to a family member telling about what you did during the day. Before going to bed, deliver the note to your family member and sit down and read it aloud.

▶ Solve each problem. Print the answer above the correct letter at the bottom. Place the correct symbol (<, >, or =) in the circle.

A. 22 + 35 = _____   **B.** 60 + 39 = _____   **C.** 50 + 31 = _____

D. 63 + 20 = _____   **E.** 10 + 3 = _____   **F.** 50 + 25 = _____

G. 77 + 7 = _____   **H.** 60 + 21 = _____   **I.** 12 + 30 = _____

1. _____ ◯ _____
    A   G

2. _____ ◯ _____
    C   H

3. _____ ◯ _____
    B   I

4. _____ ◯ _____
    F   E

5. _____ ◯ _____
    D   G

6. _____ ◯ _____
    E   H

You are the electrical inspector for your home. Walk through your home and look for electrical outlets. Each time you spot one, make a tally mark. After you have visited all the rooms, add the tally marks. What is the total number of electrical outlets in your home? Which room has the most electrical outlets?

American Education Publishing™

▶ **Read the passage. Then, answer the questions.**

Harriet Tubman

Harriet Tubman was a brave woman. She grew up as a slave in Maryland. As an adult, she escaped north to Pennsylvania. Tubman returned to Maryland to help rescue her family. She returned many times to help other slaves. She guided slaves to safety along a network known as the Underground Railroad. People who helped slaves move to freedom were called "conductors." They were named after the people who controlled trains on railroads. In 1861, the United States began fighting the Civil War. This war was partly a struggle between northern and southern states over whether people should be allowed to own slaves. President Abraham Lincoln signed a law in 1863. The law stated that slavery was no longer allowed in the United States. With the law on her side, Tubman continued for many years to help people who were treated unfairly.

1. What is the main idea of this passage?
   A. "Conductors" were people who helped slaves move to freedom.
   B. Harriet Tubman lived in Maryland.
   C. Harriet Tubman helped people on the Underground Railroad.

2. What was the Underground Railroad? _____
   _____

3. What did conductors on the Underground Railroad do? _____
   _____

You just opened a breakfast restaurant! Choose a name for your restaurant. Then, use a piece of paper and some markers to design your restaurant's breakfast menu. Share the menu with your friends. Do they want to eat breakfast at your restaurant?

▶ **Add to find each sum.**

1. 376
  + 266

2. 349
  + 233

3. 878
  + 287

4. 436
  + 296

5. 948
  + 348

6. 498
  + 439

7. 477
  + 298

8. 474
  + 396

9. 901
  + 109

10. 834
   + 249

11. 499
   + 292

12. 953
   + 118

Have an adult family member help you locate a picture of yourself when you were a baby. What do you notice about yourself in the picture? Talk with your family member about when you were a baby. What did you learn about yourself?

American Education Publishing™

▶ **Use commas, and add, remove, or rearrange words to combine the sentences.**

EXAMPLE:

I like my friends Wendy and Pete. I also like Mandy and Joe.

I like my friends Wendy, Pete, Mandy, and Joe.

1. Dogs and cats can be pets. Gerbils and hamsters can be pets too.

   _____

   _____

2. I am wearing blue jeans and a striped shirt. My shoes are black, and my socks are green. On my head is a baseball cap.

   _____

   _____

You are the help-the-birds ambassador for your neighborhood. Make a poster letting your neighbors know ways to help local birds. Include ideas for helping birds, such as building birdhouses and bird feeders.

▶ **Write the name of each shape.**

1.

   _____

2.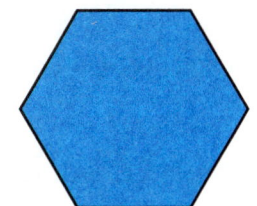

   _____

3.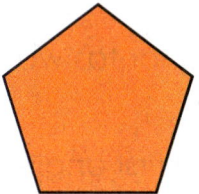

   _____

4.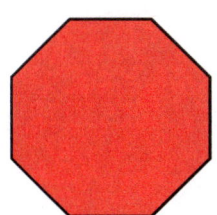

   _____

5.

   _____

6.

   _____

Make a list of all the snack foods in your family's kitchen. Read the list and ask your family members to identify their favorite snack food. Make tally marks to keep track of the responses. Which snack food is your family's favorite? Share the results with your family.

▶ **Draw three lines beneath each letter that should be capitalized.**

Pocahontas

pocahontas was an American Indian who lived in virginia during the time of the first english settlement of america. According to legend, pocahontas saved the life of captain john smith. Later, she moved to jamestown and took the name rebecca. She married mr. john rolfe, and they traveled to england to meet king james. pocahontas died in england and was buried there. She had one son, thomas.

Be your family's refrigerator inspector. Check the seal, the long rubber strip on the edge of the door. See if there is any food or dirt stuck in the seal. If so, cold air from inside the refrigerator might be getting out. Clean the seal with a wet sponge. With a clean seal, you will be helping your family save energy!

▶ **Write the word from the word bank that matches each description.**

knead	sense	praise	certain
wheat	purchase	numb	guide

1. unable to feel _____

2. we do this to dough _____

3. sure of something _____

4. to buy something _____

5. to see, hear, feel, taste, or smell _____

6. flour is made from this _____

7. a leader of a group _____

8. to express approval _____

You just received a chore that is not on your list of favorite things to do. Make a five-panel comic strip showing how you might get a family member to assist you with the job. Does your comic strip help motivate you to get your job done?

▶ **Follow the directions below to create a compassion collage.**

Compassion is seeing that someone needs help or understanding, and offering him support. Create a compassion collage. Think about ways that people show compassion. Cut out compassion pictures and words from magazines and newspapers. Use markers, poster board, and glue to create your collage. Draw small pictures, write words, and add stickers to the collage. Give your collage a title, such as *The C's of Compassion: Care, Concern, Consider*. Display the collage so that others can see how you have captured compassion.

Make a list of the rooms in your home. Look at the rooms and write the colors you see on the walls. After visiting each room, make a diagram of your home. Indicate on the diagram the color of each room. Is there a color that shows up more often than any other color?

▶ **Add to find each sum.**

1. 566
  + 467

2. 979
  + 354

3. 945
  + 379

4. 888
  + 276

5. 871
  + 739

6. 655
  + 478

7. 675
  + 597

8. 456
  + 327

9. 347
  + 254

10. 493
   + 349

11. 623
   + 387

12. 402
   + 599

Organize a neighborhood pet parade! Take a sheet of construction paper and markers and design an invitation for the event. Will there be a theme for the parade? Will pets be dressed in costumes? After designing the invitation, share it with a friend.

▶ **Draw three lines beneath each letter that should be capitalized.**

july 1, 2010

dear aunt Laura,

Thank you so much for the gift card! I'm going to use it to buy a game i've been wanting. When you and uncle Mike come to visit this summer, we can all play my new game together.

your nephew,

Blake

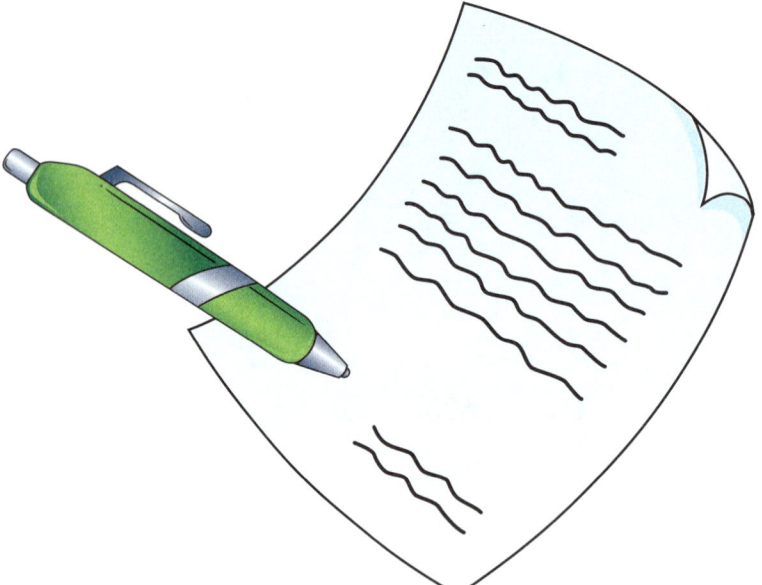

You have $20.00 to take a grandparent to lunch. Decide on a restaurant where you would like to go. Then, make a list of what you and your grandparent will order. Estimate the cost of each item. Then add it all up. Would you have enough money to pay for the lunch?

▶ **Add to find each sum.**

1. 348
 + 238

2. 349
 + 233

3. 948
 + 434

4. 869
 + 572

5. 749
 + 458

6. 638
 + 422

7. 539
 + 468

8. 578
 + 396

9. 955
 + 134

10. 768
 + 294

11. 627
 + 318

12. 587
 + 199

You and your family are going on a day trip. Where would you like to go? How would you get there? What would you see? Write a journal entry about the imaginary trip. Share your day-trip journal with a family member.

▶ **Add commas where they belong in each sentence.**

EXAMPLE:

August 10, 1970, and May 10, 1973, are birth dates in our family.

1. My parents were married in Portland Oregon on May 1 1999.

2. We had chicken potatoes corn gravy and ice cream for dinner.

3. George Washington became the first U.S. president on April 30 1789.

4. Sam was born on June 16 1947 in Rome Italy.

5. We saw deer bears elk and goats on our trip.

6. On July 24 1962 in Boise Idaho I won the big race.

Ask an adult family member to show you the water heater in your home. Feel the side of the water heater. If it feels warm, some heat is escaping and wasting energy. You may want to plan a trip to the hardware store and get an insulating blanket to wrap around the water heater.

▶ **Present-tense verbs** describe what is happening now. **Past-tense verbs** describe what happened in the past. Write a verb to complete each sentence. If there is an **n** beside the line, write a present-tense verb. If there is a **p** beside the line, write a past-tense verb.

1. Two dogs (p) _____ down the road.

2. The wind (n) _____ and the trees (n) _____ .

3. We can (n) _____ and (n) _____ in the race.

4. Last night, I (p) _____ past your house.

5. I (p) _____ at the jokes on TV last night.

6. Yesterday, we (p) _____ tulips and roses.

Take a pen and a notebook outside and find a place to sit. For a few minutes, just sit and listen. What do you hear? Close your eyes and continue to listen. What do you hear now? Make a list of things you hear. How many things did you hear?

▶ **In the story below, circle each letter that should be a capital letter. Then, add an ending to the story.**

my birthday

today is my birthday. i am nine years old. i was born on wednesday, april 12, in billings, montana. my family will celebrate my birthday tonight. mom will cook her special spaghetti dinner just for me. dad will be home from work early. my brother, david, and my sister, rose, will be here too. after dinner grandma and grandpa will come. we will all eat cake and ice cream. they will sing "happy birthday" to me. then, i . . .

_____
_____
_____
_____
_____
_____
_____

Your job is to entertain four-year-old twins by reading stories to them. Make a list of books that you think the twins would enjoy. Share your list with an older family member. Ask her to help you add books to the list and then decide on the best books for four-year-olds.

▶ **Complete each sentence by writing** *more than*, *less than*, **or** *equal to*.

> 2 cups = 1 pint   2 pints = 1 quart   4 quarts = 1 gallon

1. 2 pints are _____ 1 quart.

2. 1 gallon is _____ 1 pint.

3. 1 pint is _____ 1 quart.

4. 6 pints are _____ 3 quarts.

5. 3 quarts are _____ 1 gallon.

6. 2 pints are _____ 4 cups.

7. 5 cups are _____ 1 quart.

8. 8 quarts are _____ 2 gallons.

Go to the grocery store with an adult family member. Take a pencil and paper with you. Watch for items that are on the shopping list and on sale. As you go up and down the aisles, look for sale items. Make a list of these items and share them with your family member. What items are good buys for your family?

▶ **Write the correct word from the word bank to answer each question.**

night	hopped	numb
different	dry	knock

1. Which word begins with a silent letter?
   _____

2. Which word has the *t* sound at the end, but the letter *t* is not making the sound?
   _____

3. Which word has a silent *gh*?
   _____

4. Which word has a silent letter at the end?
   _____

5. Which word has three syllables?
   _____

6. Which word ends with the long *i* sound?
   _____

Fold a sheet of paper into an airplane. Send your airplane on several flights, measuring the distance after each throw and writing it down. How many times did you fly the paper airplane? What was the longest flight?

▶ **Read the passage. Then, answer the questions.**

Roberto Clemente

Roberto Clemente was born in Puerto Rico in 1934. He played baseball in his neighborhood as a child. Then, he played for his high school team. He joined a junior national league when he was 16. He played baseball briefly in Canada before signing to play for the Pittsburgh Pirates in 1954. Clemente served in the U.S. Marine Reserves for several years. That helped him grow stronger physically. He helped the Pirates win two World Series. During the off-season, Clemente often went back to Puerto Rico to help people. He liked visiting children in hospitals to give them hope that they could get well. An earthquake hit the country of Nicaragua in 1972. At age 38, Clemente died in an airplane crash on his way to deliver supplies to Nicaragua. He was elected to the Baseball Hall of Fame in 1973. He was the first Hispanic player to receive that honor.

1. What is the main idea of this passage?
    A. Roberto Clemente was a great baseball player who also helped people.
    B. Roberto Clemente died in an airplane crash.
    C. Roberto Clemente was elected to the Baseball Hall of Fame.

2. What happened in Nicaragua in 1972?

   _____

   _____

3. Why was Clemente flying to Nicaragua?

   _____

   _____

Write a song promoting bicycle safety. Take a pencil and paper and write the lyrics. Then, think of a good melody. Practice singing the song and then share it with family members. Is it a hit?

▶ **Solve each word problem.**

1. How many days are between the 18th and 28th day of the month?

2. Tony is next to last in line. He is also 10th from the 1st person in line. How many people are in line?

3. If today is June 22, what date will it be one week from today?

4. Jack is 16th in line. How many people are ahead of him?

Go with a family member to a nearby park. Take a pencil and notebook with you. Find a place to sit and observe the park environment. Make a list of the various things you see happening in the park. Write a summary of the park's activities. Use words that will encourage others to visit the park!

▶ The **subject** of a sentence is whom or what the sentence is about. The **predicate** of a sentence tells something about the subject. Both can have one or more words. Circle the subject and underline the predicate of each sentence.

EXAMPLE:

(Our team) <u>won the game.</u>

1. We went on a picnic.
2. A little red fox ran past us.
3. Some birds make nests for their eggs.
4. Clowns make me laugh.
5. The king rode a bike.
6. April lost her house keys.
7. Lee auditioned for the school play.
8. We started to swim.
9. The frog hopped onto the lily pad.
10. Lions live in groups called prides.
11. Olivia's mom baked the pie.
12. Noah worked in his garden.
13. I finished the book yesterday.
14. Mom and I rode our horses.

Collect your family's recyclable paper. Walk around your home and gather all the recyclable paper you find. Then, place it on a scale and weigh it. How much does it weigh? Share the results with your family members. Are they amazed?

▶ **Subtract to find each difference.**

1. 62
  − 19

2. 27
  − 18

3. 45
  − 38

4. 73
  − 19

5. 42
  − 29

6. 19
  − 9

7. 86
  − 57

8. 66
  − 59

9. 44
  − 26

10. 53
  − 14

11. 91
  − 73

12. 33
  − 26

Create a funny four-panel comic strip. Think of a funny situation that might happen at home, perhaps in the kitchen. Then, take a sheet of paper and markers and create a funny comic strip. Share your comic strip with family members. Did it make them smile?

▶ **Write the correct present-tense form of the verb *be* to complete each sentence.**

1. Mona _____ my next door neighbor.

2. You _____ a great friend.

3. I _____ the oldest child in my family.

4. Bill and Shelby _____ at the movies.

5. I _____ at my aunt's house.

6. You _____ very helpful today.

7. Pizza _____ my favorite food.

Take a pencil and notebook and find a place where you can safely observe the traffic in your neighborhood. Make a list of the different colors of cars you see. Use tally marks for multiple viewings of the same color cars. Add the tally marks for each color. What color car did you see the most often? The least?

▶ **Solve each word problem. Show your work.**

1. Taylor's mom volunteered at the face-painting booth. She started with 14 tubes of face paint. At the end of the festival, she had 7 tubes left. How many tubes did she use during the festival?

2. Sean scored 5 baskets in the free throw contest. His friend Joshua scored 9 baskets. How many more baskets did Joshua score than Sean?

3. Twelve teachers sat in the dunking booth to raise money for new library books. Nine of them were dunked. How many teachers were not dunked?

4. At the end of the festival, Alexis noticed that she had 2 tickets left. If she started the festival with 10 tickets, how many tickets did she use?

Decide on one activity you would like to do this summer. Then, write a note convincing an adult family member that this activity is something you should be permitted to do very soon. Share the note with the adult family member. How does he respond?

▶ **Circle the word that does not belong in each group of words. Then, describe why the other words belong together.**

1. tuba, clarinet, jazz, flute, harp _____
   _____

2. tire, hammer, screwdriver, wrench _____
   _____

3. robin, hawk, sparrow, dog, crow _____
   _____

4. Moon, Mars, Earth, Jupiter, Venus _____
   _____

5. lettuce, peach, carrot, peas, beets _____
   _____

6. rose, daisy, lazy, tulip, lily _____
   _____

During the early morning hours, go outside with an adult family member. Find a place to sit and observe the world. Use a pencil and paper to list the sounds you hear. How many different sounds do you hear? What is the loudest sound? What is the softest sound?

▶ **Subtract to find each difference.**

1. 64
   − 57

2. 23
   − 9

3. 70
   − 23

4. 43
   − 14

5. 63
   − 45

6. 91
   − 42

7. 38
   − 19

8. 81
   − 15

9. 55
   − 9

10. 42
    − 27

11. 75
    − 18

12. 27
    − 19

Farmers' markets are popular during the summer months. They provide an opportunity for people to buy fresh produce directly from farmers. Create a 30-second commercial for a local farmers' market. Share your commercial with family members, friends, and neighbors.

▶ **Complete each sentence with the future-tense form of the verb in parentheses.**

1. Maria _____ dinner tonight.
   (cook)

2. Angelo _____ his stepmother this weekend.
   (visit)

3. Carrie _____ to the movies tomorrow.
   (go)

4. Scott _____ his new book this evening.
   (read)

5. Wendy _____ me her new bracelet when she returns.
   (show)

It takes practice to develop the art of pantomime. Decide on a morning activity that could be pantomimed, such as brushing your teeth. Practice the pantomime and then share it with family members. Did they recognize what you were pantomiming?

▶ **Solve each problem.**

1. 6.34
   − 2.68

2. 9.87
   + 4.89

3. 4.93
   − 2.77

4. 8.88
   + 2.76

5. 7.32
   − 2.99

6. 9.47
   + 2.76

7. 4.96
   + 3.94

8. 5.57
   − 3.23

9. 3.47
   + 2.54

10. 9.45
    − 6.37

11. 3.65
    + 2.19

12. 4.73
    − 2.46

Make a list of questions to ask your adult family members about what they remember about being your age. Ask the questions and then share what you learn with your family.

▶ **Add a suffix to each word. Use -*est*, -*tion*, or -*ty*. Double, drop, or change some letters if needed.**

EXAMPLE:

tasty _____*tastiest*_____

1. sad _____
2. act _____
3. direct _____
4. safe _____
5. dirt _____
6. hungry _____
7. invent _____
8. prepare _____
9. happy _____
10. honest _____

Make a three-panel comic strip showing what you would like to have for dinner. Include a main course, a side dish, and a dessert. Post your comic strip for your family members to see.

▶ **Solve each problem.**

1. 7.42
   − 1.16

2. 8.70
   − 6.30

3. 3.69
   − 1.25

4. 9.60
   + 1.92

5. 575
   − 162

6. 600
   + 197

7. 804
   + 129

8. 133
   − 124

9. 202
   − 102

10. 7.34
    − 5.17

11. 525
    + 417

12. 762
    − 126

Make your room a healthier place by adding some plants. Plants purify the air. Ask an adult family member if there is a plant in your home that you can put in your room. You might even want to make the plant feel welcome in your room by decorating its pot. Where is a good place to put the plant?

▶ The words *is* and *are* tell that something is happening now. Use *is* with singular subjects and *are* with plural subjects. Write *is* or *are* to correctly complete each sentence.

1. Max and I _____ best friends.

2. Bill _____ visiting his grandparents this week.

3. We _____ going camping at the lake.

4. Megan _____ biking with her friend Toni.

5. Her sister _____ in the eighth grade.

6. Those bananas _____ very ripe.

7. That book _____ one of my favorites.

8. Hugo and Malia _____ bringing snacks to the party.

Be captain of your home battery team! Take paper and pencil and walk around your home. Make a list of everything you find that uses batteries. Share the results with family members. Talk about which items you might possibly do without.

▶ **Subtract to find each difference.**

1. 300
   −130

2. 510
   −250

3. 804
   −163

4. 905
   −662

5. 404
   −142

6. 623
   −257

7. 771
   −704

8. 900
   −156

9. 435
   −297

10. 278
    −126

11. 829
    −536

12. 379
    −208

At the end of the day, write a note to yourself telling about the good things you did during the day. Before going to bed, share the note with a family member and then talk with him about the good things he did that day.

▶ **Follow the direcions below to impove your flexibility.**

Did you know that a backyard game of catch can improve your flexibility? Find a friend or family member and a variety of balls, such as a tennis ball, baseball, softball, or foam ball. Throw each ball back and forth. As you throw, concentrate on extending your front foot and throwing arm. As this gets easier, increase the distance between yourself and your partner. For a challenge, try throwing with your other hand. This will be harder, but it will give both sides of your body equal stretching time. As you throw, remember to "stretch" your limits!

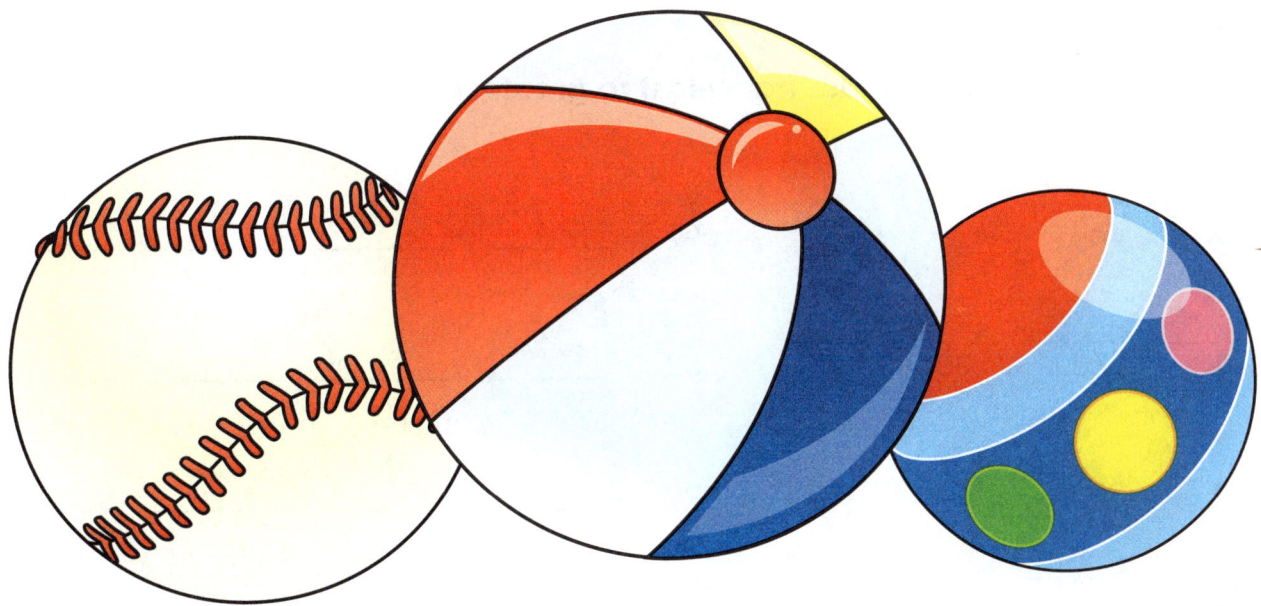

Think of good deeds you can do to surprise your family members. Use paper and a pencil to make a list of your family members. Next to each name, write a simple good deed that you can do for each of them. Then, begin quietly doing your good deeds. Remember, it is a good-deed surprise!

American Education Publishing™

▶ **Write the numbers in order from greatest to least.**

1. 261   325   496   547   _____ _____ _____ _____

2. 746   793   733   779   _____ _____ _____ _____

3. 596   579   488   499   _____ _____ _____ _____

4. 496   649   964   946   _____ _____ _____ _____

▶ **Write the numbers in order from least to greatest.**

5. 764   674   746   647   _____ _____ _____ _____

6. 503   530   353   550   _____ _____ _____ _____

7. 940   579   488   499   _____ _____ _____ _____

8. 496   649   964   946   _____ _____ _____ _____

Go on a coin scavenger hunt! Look for coins that may have fallen out of someone's pocket and are hidden from view. Look under a chair or couch cushion or under a piece of furniture. Make a list of each type of coin you find. Count the money. Was it worth going on the scavenger hunt?

Read the story. Then, answer the questions.

Photograph

Jack was not comfortable. His new shirt was too stiff and his tie felt tight. Mother had fussed over his hair, trying to get it to look just right. She made him scrub his hands three times to remove the dirt from under his fingernails! Finally, his mom said he was ready. She smiled and said that Jack looked very handsome. Jack frowned, but he knew he could not tell his mom how he felt. This was important to her. Jack sat on a special stool that turned, and he looked at the camera. He did not feel like smiling, but he did his best. "Perfect!" said the man behind the camera as he snapped the shot. Jack posed two more times, and then the man said they were finished. The first thing Jack did was take off his tie!

1. What was Jack doing? _____
   _____
   _____

2. What clues tell you where Jack is? _____
   _____
   _____

3. What clues tell you how Jack feels? _____
   _____
   _____

Have you or a family member lost something recently? Hunt down the lost item. Take paper and markers and make a "wanted" poster. Draw a picture of the item and write a description of it. Include when and where it was last seen. Place the poster where family members can view it and help locate the missing object.

▶ **Subtract to find each difference.**

1. 3.01
   − 2.42

2. 5.41
   − 3.77

3. 4.71
   − 3.82

4. 7.27
   − 4.19

5. 8.48
   − 3.99

6. 8.47
   − 3.58

7. 5.02
   − 3.21

8. 7.04
   − 6.67

9. 8.46
   − 4.57

10. 2.11
    − 1.97

11. 9.16
    − 2.37

12. 6.07
    − 4.28

Help your family save energy by being a refrigerator friend! Take paper and markers and make yourself a badge that says, "Refrigerator Friend." Then, post a sign on your refrigerator reminding your family members to wait for food to cool before putting it into the refrigerator.

▶ **Read the story. Then, write four details from the story in the order that they occurred.**

Washing Dad's Car

Quinn and Phillip washed their dad's car. First, they filled a bucket with soapy water. Quinn got some old rags from the house while Phillip got the hose. They put soapy water all over the car and wiped off the dirt. Next, they rinsed the car with water. To finish the job, Quinn and Phillip dried the car with some clean towels. They were both surprised when their dad gave them $5 each.

1. They filled a bucket of soapy water.

2. Then, Quinn got old raggs while Phillip got the hose.

3. They put the soapy water all over the car and got the dirt off.

4. Next, they rinsed the car with water. To finsh the job, Quinn and Phillp dried the car with clean rags.

Does your family like music? If so, what kind? Interview each family member about her taste in music. Then, create a report on your family's favorite music. Write a 30-second news spot highlighting your family's musical preferences. Then, share your news report with your family.

▶ **Add to find each sum.**

1. 38.78
  + 84.56

2. 96.75
  + 42.83

3. 32.34
  + 46.52

4. 89.00
  + 39.57

5. 92.31
  + 53.32

6. 85.69
  + 25.46

7. 74.58
  + 54.94

8. 23.43
  + 73.28

9. 48.02
  + 36.89

Make food sculptures from pretzels, gumdrops, licorice, raisins, cream cheese, peanut butter, and so on. Make a shopping list of items that you would like to use in your food sculpture. Remember, the last thing you do as the creator of the food sculpture is eat it!

▶ Each word below contains the suffix -*est*, -*tion*, or -*ty*. Circle each suffix. Then, write the base word.

EXAMPLE:

safe(ty) _____ *safe* _____

1. saddest _____
2. hungriest _____
3. preparation _____
4. invention _____
5. tasty _____
6. certainty _____
7. loyalty _____
8. direction _____
9. loveliest _____
10. surest _____

Go with a family member to a nearby park. Take a bird book with you. Find a place to sit and observe the birds in the park. Talk with your family member about the different birds you observe and find them in the bird book. What different kinds of birds do you see?

▶ **Add to find each sum.**

1. 246
 + 129

2. 500
 + 806

3. 924
 + 289

4. 402
 + 629

5. 1,284
 + 2,629

6. 7,762
 + 1,473

7. 3,383
 + 5,007

8. 4,290
 + 2,968

9. 9,542
 + 695

Tour your home and write down each room that has a door. Select one of the rooms on your list. Draw a picture of the door, showing your new decorating plan. Share your door design with family members. Do they like your design?

▶ Read the passage. Then, answer the questions.

Lucy Maud Montgomery

Lucy Maud Montgomery is famous for creating the character of Anne Shirley in the Anne of Green Gables series. Montgomery was born in 1874 on Prince Edward Island in Canada. She lived with her grandparents and went to class in a one-room schoolhouse. Her first poem was published when she was 17 years old. She wrote *Anne of Green Gables* in 1905, but it was not published until 1908. The book became a best-seller, and Montgomery wrote several other books based on the main character. Two films and at least seven TV shows have been made from the Anne of Green Gables series. Although Montgomery moved away from Prince Edward Island in 1911, all but one of her books are set there. Many people still visit the island today to see where Anne Shirley grew up.

1. What is the main idea of this passage?
   A. Lucy Maud Montgomery grew up on Prince Edward Island.
   B. Lucy Maud Montgomery is famous for writing *Anne of Green Gables*.
   C. Lucy Maud Montgomery was a schoolteacher.

2. Who is Anne Shirley? _____

3. What was Montgomery's early life like? _____
   _____

4. How can you tell that *Anne of Green Gables* was a popular book?
   _____

Make a two-column chart, labeling one column "Family Member" and the other column "Number of Glasses of Water." Post the chart near where family members get glasses of water and ask them to make a tally mark next to their name each time they get a glass of water. At the end of the day, find out the total number of glasses of water your family consumed. Which family member drank the most water?

▶ **Add to find each sum.**

1. 3,878
   4,981
   + 8,165

2. 9,651
   3,321
   + 2,283

3. 3,981
   2,357
   + 4,652

4. 76
   59
   + 53

5. 34
   67
   + 24

6. 776
   453
   + 719

7. 5,349
   3,274
   + 7,184

8. 676
   734
   + 651

9. 7,028
   4,354
   + 5,684

Use paper and colored pencils to make a three-panel comic strip showing different ways you stay cool during the summer. Share your comic strip with family members and friends. Do they do the same things, or do they have other ways to stay cool?

▶ **Write the past-tense form of each underlined verb.**

1. A tadpole <u>hatches</u> from an egg in a pond. _____

2. He <u>looks</u> like a small fish at first. _____

3. The tadpole <u>uses</u> his tail to swim. _____

4. He <u>breathes</u> with gills. _____

5. His appearance <u>changes</u> after a few weeks. _____

6. He <u>starts</u> to grow hind legs. _____

7. His head <u>flattens</u>. _____

8. His gills <u>vanish</u>. _____

9. His tail <u>disappears</u>. _____

10. He <u>hops</u> onto dry land. _____

Take a trip to a world-famous zoo! Where is this zoo located? How would you get there? What animals would you see? Use paper and markers to design a zoo postcard. Then, write a note to your family telling them about your zoo visit. Share the postcard with family members.

▶ **Get a dictionary. Choose any page between 40 and 55. Then, follow the directions.**

1. Write the guide words for that page.

   _____

2. Write the meaning of the guide word that is on the right.

   _____

   _____

3. How many syllables does the guide word on the left have?

   _____

4. What mark is used to show how words are divided into syllables?

   _____

5. Guide words show the _____ and the _____ words on the page.

Be your family's repurposer. Locate old greeting cards and a pair of scissors. You can reuse the greeting cards by cutting them into gift tags. Store them where they will be easily available at gift-giving time.

▶ **Add to find each sum.**

1.   4,340
     5,433
   + 3,238

2.   356
      674
    + 380

3.   54
      39
    + 73

4.   634
      198
    + 518

5.   67
      98
    + 74

6.   47
      34
    + 99

7.   321
      436
    + 548

8.   2,783
     2,546
   + 6,748

    9,418
    8,009
  + 7,245

Create a commercial about your favorite book. Make a list of three books you have really enjoyed reading. Then, select one and write a 30-second commercial about it. Share your commercial with your friends.

▶ **Clipped words** are short versions of longer words. Write the clipped word for each underlined word.

EXAMPLE:

Upton ate a <u>hamburger</u> and fruit for lunch. _____burger_____

1. When Ryan grows up, he wants to fly <u>airplanes</u>. _____

2. A <u>hippopotamus</u> can hold her breath for a long time. _____

3. Have you ever been inside a <u>submarine</u>? _____

4. Lori loves talking with her grandmother on the <u>telephone</u>. _____

5. Matt was amazed by the <u>photograph</u> in the art gallery. _____

Go to the grocery store with an adult family member. Take a pencil and paper with you. Imagine that you have $5.00 to spend. What three items can you find that have a total cost of under $5.00?

▶ **Add to find each sum.**

1. 6,898
   5,433
   + 2,154

2. 8,459
   4,908
   + 4,356

3. 525
   653
   + 896

4. 5,265
   2,278
   + 8,365

5. 2,147
   3,255
   + 2,256

6. 654
   452
   + 138

7. 7,092
   5,405
   + 6,124

8. 5,768
   6,937
   + 7,034

9. 4,265
   5,124
   + 6,489

Take markers and a notebook outside and find a place to sit. Observe the trees and shrubs. Note the different shapes and sizes of the trees and shrubs. Draw pictures of what you see. Share your pictures with family members. Can they help you identify the different kinds of trees and shrubs?

American Education Publishing™

▶ **Read the passage. Then, answer the questions.**

Elisha Otis

Have you ever ridden in an elevator? Elevators make it much easier for people to get from one floor to another in a tall building. At one time, elevators were not as safe as they are today. Elisha Otis helped change that. Early elevators used ropes that sometimes broke, sending the people riding the elevator to the ground. To make elevators safer, Otis made wooden guide rails to go on each side of an elevator. Cables ran through the rails and were connected to a spring that would pull the elevator up if the cables broke. Otis displayed his invention for the first time at the New York Crystal Palace Exhibition in 1853. His safety elevators were used in buildings as tall as the Eiffel Tower in Paris, France, and the Empire State Building in New York City, New York. Otis died in 1861. His sons, Charles and Norton, continued to sell his design, and many elevators today still have the Otis name on them.

1. What is the main idea of this passage?
   A. The Otis family still sells elevators today.
   B. At one time, elevators were unsafe to use.
   C. Elisha Otis found a way to make elevators safe.

2. Why were early elevators dangerous? _____
   _____

3. What did the spring in Otis's elevators do? _____
   _____

4. When and where was Otis's elevator displayed for the first time? _____
   _____

Imagine a summer day when you do not have a television, a computer, video games, or a phone. Make a list of five things you would do. Share the list with a family member. Together, add five more things to the list. Then, choose one of the items on the list and do it!

▶ **Fill in the blanks to complete the friendly letter. Use correct capitalization.**

_____ (date)

_____ , (greeting)

    I'm having a _____ summer. So far, the best part of the summer has been _____

_____

_____

_____

_____

_____ , (closing)

_____ (your name)

Which window in your home gives you the best view of the outdoors? Take paper and markers and go look out that window. Draw a picture of what you see. Show your picture to a family member. Talk about the picture and how it might look in the winter.

▶ Read each verb. Write **A** if it is a present-tense action verb. Write **L** if it is a linking verb.

EXAMPLES:

___*a*___ bloom   ___*L*___ is

1. _____ has   2. _____ hatch

3. _____ have   4. _____ appears

5. _____ pretend   6. _____ stir

7. _____ becomes   8. _____ study

9. _____ walk   10. _____ hold

11. _____ were   12. _____ am

13. _____ skip   14. _____ was

"Have fun and play the day away" is the slogan for the day. Create a song encouraging others to join you in having fun and playing. Share your song with family and friends. Are they ready to have fun too?

▶ **Solve each problem.**

1.   4,936
   + 5,432

2.   9,675
   − 4,283

3.   5,349
   + 6,393

4.   6,434
   − 6,398

5.   754
   − 528

6.   751
   − 439

7.   8,236
   − 5,548

8.   7,840
   − 4,251

9.   6,324
   − 3,489

Go on a scavenger hunt around your home. Look for recyclable plastic bottles and containers. Make a list of the recyclable items you find. Does your family currently recycle plastic bottles and containers? If not, how might you begin a family recycling program?

▶ **Read each pair of sentences. Circle the letter of the sentence that shows the future tense.**

1. A. Mischa ran to the market.
   B. Mischa will run around the block.

2. A. I am having green beans with dinner.
   B. I will have corn tomorrow.

3. A. Troy will catch the ball.
   B. Troy catches the ball.

4. A. He will go to the new school.
   B. He went to the new school.

5. A. Davion washed the dog.
   B. Davion will wash the dog.

Summer days tend to be warm and sometimes get very hot. Talk with an adult family member about ways your home is kept cooler in hot weather. Together, can you think of at least five ways?

▶ **Subtract to find each difference.**

1. 943
   − 549

2. 7,452
   − 6,789

3. 526
   − 268

4. 526
   − 498

5. 754
   − 528

6. 751
   − 439

7. 8,236
   − 5,548

8. 7,840
   − 4,251

9. 6,324
   − 3,489

You are going to ride in your city's bicycle parade! How might you decorate your bike? Use items around the house to make decorations. Do not forget to decorate your helmet!

▶ **Follow the directions to draw a picture in the box.**

1. Draw a tree in the bottom left corner with four branches and orange and red leaves.
2. Draw a yellow half moon in the upper right corner.
3. Draw a brown fence across the bottom.
4. Draw four gray cats on the fence.
5. Draw six dark clouds in the sky.
6. Draw one owl on a branch of the tree.
7. Draw five black birds flying in the sky.
8. Add any other details you wish.

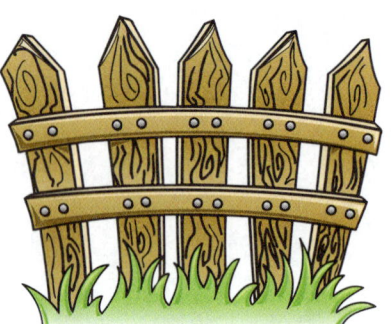

Play lunchtime chef and surprise a family member with lunch! Quietly go to the kitchen with an adult family member and look at the lunch possibilities. Decide on the menu and then create it. In what special way might you serve the surprise lunch?

▶ **How can colors be separated?**

Chromatography is a process used to separate colors. This activity shows how part of the ink in water-soluble markers can be dissolved. Other, more soluble colors will travel up a coffee filter with water.

Materials:
- 3 water-soluble markers (not permanent markers)
- 3 drinking glasses
- coffee filter
- masking tape
- scissors
- ruler
- water

Procedure:
Pour water into each glass so that it is about a half-inch (1.3 cm) deep. Label each glass and marker *1*, *2*, or *3* using masking tape and the markers. Cut the coffee filter into three strips, one for each marker. Use the water-soluble markers to make one large dot one-third of the way up each coffee filter strip. Do this for all three markers. Place each coffee filter strip in the glass with the same number as the marker. The ink dots should be near, but not under, the water. Let the strips absorb the water.

1. What happened to the ink dots as the coffee filter strips absorbed water?

   _____

   _____

2. What happened differently to each of the three different ink dots?

   _____

   _____

Invent a new circus act! The new act will include you along with another person. Write an ad describing the act and the talents needed. Share your ad with family members. Are any of them willing to join the circus?

▶ **Subtract to find each difference. Regroup if needed.**

1. 5,042
   − 1,624

2. 2,710
   − 1,624

3. 4,200
   − 1,122

4. 7,106
   − 2,410

5. 3,340
   − 1,112

6. 9,824
   − 1,224

7. 6,831
   − 4,560

8. 7,605
   − 1,282

9. 6,351
   − 5,675

Ask an adult family member to join you on a hunt for four-leaf clovers. Talk about a good place to hunt for four-leaf clovers and then schedule a time to go. How many four-leaf clovers did you find?

▶ **How is the height of a ramp related to the speed of a toy?**

Kinetic energy is the energy of motion. Potential energy is stored energy, or the energy of position.

Materials:
- ruler
- toy car
- stopwatch
- wooden ramp of any size

Procedure:

Raise one end of the ramp to the lowest height (about 1.5 inches [4 cm]) required for the toy car to roll from one end to the other. Place the car at the top of the ramp and use the stopwatch to time it as it rolls to the bottom of the ramp. Record the speed of the car and the height of the ramp on the chart below. Repeat the activity two more times, raising the height of the ramp each time.

Trial	Height	Time
1		
2		
3		

1. What is the relationship between the height of the ramp and the speed of the object? _____
   _____

2. What surfaces might cause the toy car to roll faster or slower? _____
   _____

Design your own summer wardrobe. To get started, take scissors and some old catalogs. Look for clothing items you would like to have in your closet. Cut them out and then share them with your family. Do they like your summer wardrobe?

▶ **Complete each multiplication chart.**

1.

× 2	
4	
8	
3	6
6	
9	
5	10
7	

2.

× 3	
3	9
7	
5	
2	
6	18
4	
8	

3.

× 4	
10	
5	20
8	
4	
7	
6	
9	

4.

× 5	
9	
2	
6	
3	15
5	
7	
4	

Make a book of your favorite things. Take five sheets of paper. On each page, write one of the five senses at the top, then draw and label things you enjoy with that sense. Share your favorite things book with friends and family.

▶ Read the description of a map scale below.

> A **map scale** represents distance on a map. A map cannot be shown at actual size, so it must be made smaller to fit on paper. On the map below, 1 inch = 30 miles.

▶ Study the map of Lee Island. Measure the distance between towns with a ruler. Then, change the inches to miles to find the actual distance between each pair of towns. Remember, 1 inch = 30 miles.

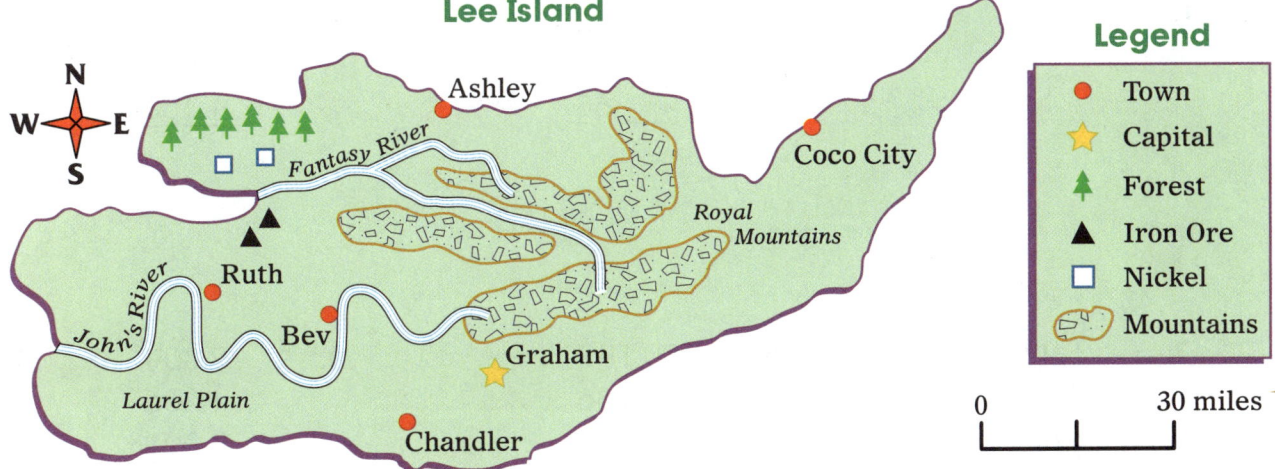

1. Ashley to Coco City _____

2. Coco City to Chandler _____

3. Graham to Bev _____

4. Ruth to Ashley _____

Make a list of all the pets you have seen in your neighborhood. Share your list with a family member. Together, rank the pets from biggest to smallest. What is the smallest pet in your neighborhood?

American Education Publishing™

▶ **Add to find each sum.**

1.   62
      + 27

2.   75
      + 85

3.   54
      + 92

4.   736
        89
      + 104

5.   3,482
        437
      + 68

6.   246
       442
      + 53

7.   6,428
      1,375
    + 3,684

8.   30,147
      25,236
    + 42,613

9.   2,804
      1,366
    + 5,391

10.   5,894
      1,388
    + 3,137

11.   28,123
      33,294
    + 46,510

12.   14,738
      22,856
    + 17,979

Imagine that instead of a summer day, it is a winter day. What are you wearing? Where are you? What are you doing? Write a journal entry telling about your day. Share your writing with a family member and a friend.

▶ **Follow the directions below to learn more about nature.**

Turn your backyard or neighborhood into a math classroom to practice estimation. Put on your gardening gloves and pick up a small clump of grass, wood chips, pine straw, or other safe, small material. Estimate how many pieces are in the group. Then, place the material on the ground and count the number of pieces in it to see how close your estimate was.

Make a relief map of an outdoor space near your home. Wear gardening gloves and use sand, mud, sticks, and other natural materials to form the physical features of the area. Shape the land features on a hard, flat surface, such as a piece of plywood or a sandbox floor. Some of the physical features may not be the usual ones found in your social studies class. Make whatever features are noticeable on the landscape's surface, such as hills, driveways, ponds, and playground equipment.

Gather a variety of natural objects, such as shells, stones, leaves, small sticks, pine straw, and bark. Use glue to attach the objects to a flat, square piece of wood or cardboard to create a natural masterpiece. Make a shape, a design, or even a scene to illustrate the beauty of the natural world.

Find a comfortable place to sit in your home. Take a blindfold and cover your eyes. Sit and listen. What do you hear? How do you feel? After some time, take off the blindfold. Write a poem about the experience. Share the poem with a family member.

▶ **Sometimes a map is drawn with a grid. The number coordinates on the map grid below are located on both sides of the map. The letter coordinates are located at the top and bottom of the map. Look at the locations of the different cities. Write the name of each city on the line beside the matching coordinates at the bottom of the page.**

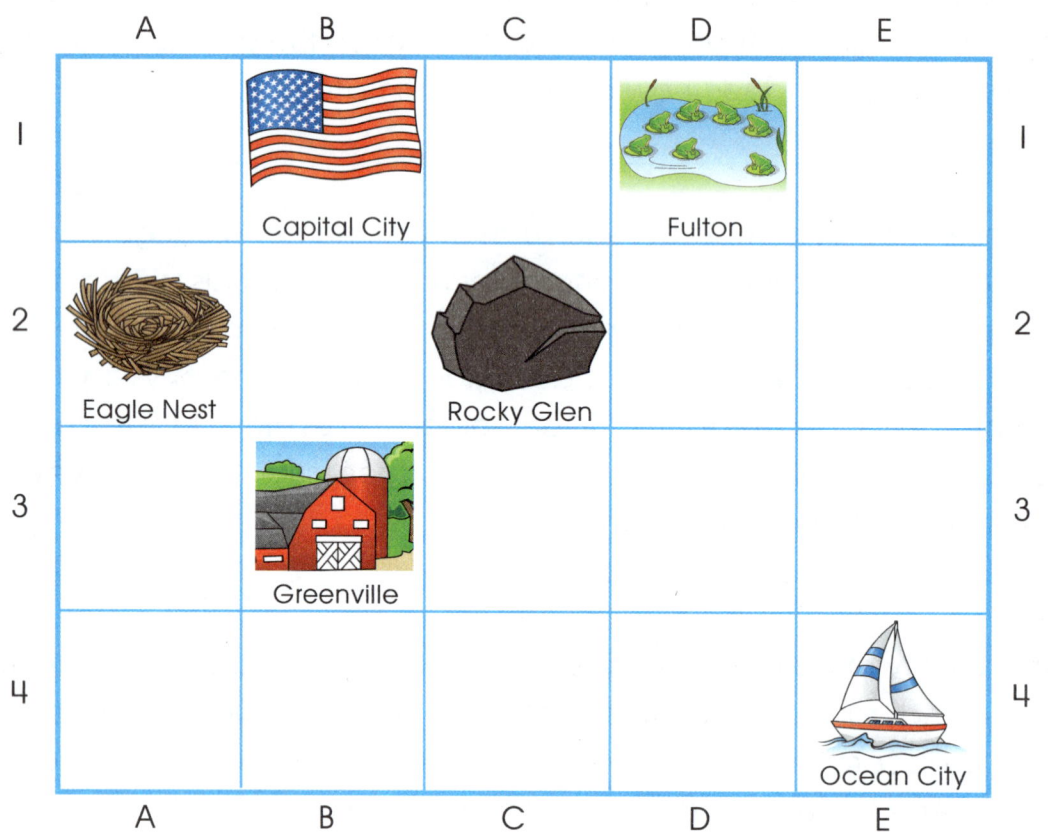

1. (D, 1) _____
2. (B, 3) _____
3. (C, 2) _____
4. (B, 1) _____
5. (A, 2) _____
6. (E, 4) _____

You are famous! People always ask for your autograph. Find a timer and set it for one minute. Pretend you are signing autographs. How many times can you write your first and last name in a minute?

▶ **Write a book report about your favorite book. Use the outline below to help you.**

Title _____

Author _____

Main characters _____

Where and when does the story take place? _____
_____

What is the main idea of the book? _____
_____
_____

Why did you like the book? _____
_____
_____
_____
_____

Look out a window and observe the weather. Then, write the lyrics for a song about today's weather. What is the mood of the song? Share your song with a family member.

American Education Publishing™

▶ **Read the story. Then, write what you think happened next on the lines below.**

A Real Monster Movie

Hannah loved monster movies. She would stay up all night to watch them. One night when there was school the next day, Hannah sneaked downstairs to watch a monster movie at three o'clock in the morning. She was very tired when she went back to bed. When her alarm went off an hour later, Hannah got up and looked in the mirror.

"Oh, no!" she said, for now she was big and green and scaly and horrible. Hannah had turned into a monster herself.

_____

_____

_____

_____

_____

_____

_____

You are the sportscaster for a big upcoming game. What kind of game is it? Who will be playing? Write your greeting for the sports fans listening to you. Then, share it with family and friends.

▶ **Quotation marks** set off what someone says. Write quotation marks in each sentence around what each person says.

EXAMPLE:

Uncle Neil said, **"**I will pack a picnic lunch.**"**

1. **"**Where is the big beach ball?**"** asked Jeff.

2. Ilene exclaimed, **"**That is a wonderful idea!**"**

3. **"**Come and do your work,**"** Grandma said, **"**or you can't go with us.**"**

4. **"**Yesterday,**"** said Ella, **"**I saw a pretty robin in the tree by my window.**"**

5. **"**I will always take care of my pets,**"** promised Theodore.

6. Rachel said, **"**Maybe we should have practiced more.**"**

7. Dr. Jacobs asked, **"**How are you, Pat?**"**

Make a list of the different ways your family uses water. Share your list with adult family members. Can they add to the list? Talk about possible ways to conserve water.

▶ **Multiply to find each product.**

1. 16
   × 5

2. 15
   × 7

3. 28
   × 3

4. 24
   × 4

5. 26
   × 4

6. 47
   × 2

7. 19
   × 4

8. 19
   × 5

9. 38
   × 2

Time for a family talent show! Make a list of family members. Next to each name, write the talent. Share your list with family members. Do they agree with your talent choices for them?

▶ **Read the questions. Then, on the lines below, write a story about a real or imaginary place you would like to visit this summer.**

Consider the following questions before you begin to write.
- Who are the characters in the story?
- Where does the story take place?
- How does the story begin?
- What happens next?
- How does the story end?

_____
_____
_____
_____
_____
_____
_____
_____
_____
_____
_____
_____

You are a well-known writer of children's books. Write a story about a family of squirrels that live in a tree near your home. Decide on the family's name and give a name to each family member. Share the squirrel character names with your family members.

▶ **Multiply to find each product.**

1. 26　　　　2.　49　　　　3.　87
  × 12　　　　　× 33　　　　　× 28

4. 51　　　　5.　94　　　　6.　81
  × 42　　　　　× 78　　　　　× 32

7. 23　　　　8.　55　　　　9.　62
  × 18　　　　　× 37　　　　　× 29

Give your family an early morning wake-up call. List five ways that you might do this. Then, ask your family members to vote on their favorite. Which wake-up call do they prefer?

▶ **Common nouns** are general names for people, places, or things. **Proper nouns** name specific people, places, or things and begin with uppercase letters. Write each noun under the correct heading.

dog	November	boat
Monday	holiday	beans
ocean	Mr. Brown	Rex
Main Street	July	apple

Common Nouns **Proper Nouns**

dog — Monday

ocean — Main Street

holiday — November

boat — Mr. Brown

beans — July

apples — Rex

The power is off. It is a hot summer day. In fact, it is the hottest day of the summer. Sketch five different ways to beat the summer heat. Poll your family members. Which way do they think is the best way to stay cool?

▶ **Read the passage. Then, answer the questions.**

Choosing a Pet

Before you decide what kind of pet you would like to own, there are some things you should think about. First, find out how much care the pet will need. Dogs need to be walked; horses need to be exercised; cats need a place to scratch. All pets need to be kept clean and well fed. You should also think about where your pet would live. Big pets need a lot of room, while little pets do not need as much room.

1. What is the topic of the passage?
    A. caring for a dog
    B. choosing a pet
    C. feeding big pets
    D. where pets live

2. What is the main idea?
    A. finding good homes for pets
    B. things to do when choosing a pet
    C. things to think about before choosing a pet
    D. bringing your pet home

Take paper and a pencil and go to your favorite place in your home. Find a comfortable spot to sit and write a poem about this place. Share your poem with family members. What is their favorite spot?

▶ **Multiply to find each product.**

RULE:
1. Multiply ones, then regroup.
2. Multiply tens, then add extra tens.
3. Multiply hundreds.
4. Regroup as needed.

EXAMPLE:

```
     1         1        2 1
   453       453      453
 x   4     x   4    x   4
 ─────     ─────    ─────
     2        12    1,812
```

1. 100
    × 3
    ───
    300

2. 120
    × 2
    ───
    240

3. ²³278
    × 4
    ────
    1082

4. ²329
    × 3
    ───
    987

5. ¹¹422
    × 5
    ────
    10

6. ²705
    × 4
    ─────
    2,820

7. ²⁶827
    × 9
    ─────
    7,443

8. ¹⁴926
    × 7
    ─────
    6483

9. ²¹652
    × 5
    ─────
    3260

Find a box. Make a sign identifying it for recyclables. Have family members vote on the best location for the box. Then, place the box in the winning location.

▶ **Write the correct homophone from the word bank to complete each sentence.**

| too | two | to | cent | scent | sent |

1. The ___two___ kittens played with the ball.

2. A penny equals one ___cent___.

3. My aunt asked me to go ___to___ the store.

4. Malcolm ___sent___ a letter to his friend.

5. I will clean my desk and the table ___too___.

6. The flower has a sweet ___scent___.

Go on a hat safari at home. Where can you find hats? Make a list of the hats you spot. How many hats do you find altogether? Which hat is your favorite? Share your hat list with family members.

▶ **Divide each set of objects into the correct number of groups.**

EXAMPLE:

Make 3 equal groups.

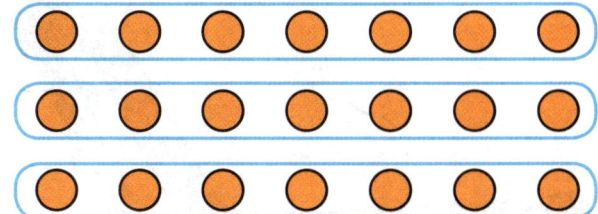

How many are in each group? __7__

1. Make 5 equal groups.

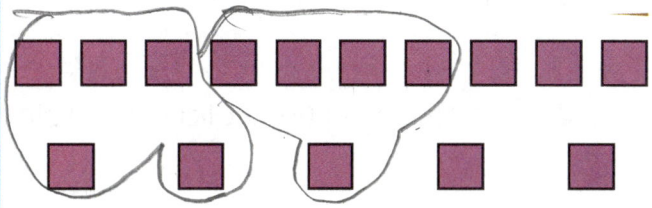

How many are in each group? _____

2. Make 2 equal groups.

How many are in each group? _____

3. Make 4 equal groups.

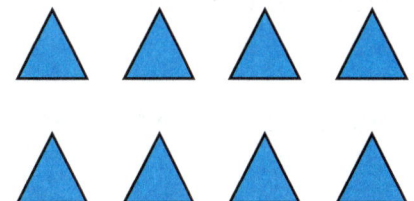

How many are in each group? _____

Design a room especially for you. Look through old catalogs. Cut out pictures of items you would like in your room. Note the price of each item and write it down. After your room design is complete, find the total cost of the room. What is it? Share the photos with adult family members. How much do they think it would cost?

▶ **Circle the articles** *a*, *an*, **and** *the* **in the sentences. Then, underline the noun that each article modifies.**

1. Our dog sleeps in (a) bed.

2. (The) movie made us laugh.

3. I carried (an) umbrella in (the) rain.

4. Our boat had (a) leak.

5. Earth rotates around (the) sun.

6. I ate (an) apple and (a) sandwich for lunch.

7. Dad keeps the nails in (an) egg carton.

8. (The) books filled (the) shelf.

9. Rick saw (a) blue whale in (the) ocean.

10. (The) elephant likes to eat peanuts.

Earn some extra money. A good business idea is to be a neighborhood pet exerciser. Take a blank card and markers and create a business card. Did you find any customers?

▶ **Read each group of words. Circle the word in each set that is spelled correctly and write it on the line.**

1. wunderful   (wonderful)   wondirful   — wonderful
2. (warm)   wirm   warme   — warm
3. wurried   woried   (worried)   — worried
4. woh   hwo   (who)   — who
5. wair   (where)   wher   — where
6. (weigh)   weh   wiegh   — weigh
7. wint   wat   (want)   — want
8. w'ont   (won't)   wo'nt   — won't

You are a caterer. You just made a delicious lunch for one of your customers and are ready to deliver it. Write a receipt for the catered lunch. Include the cost for each item and the total cost. Show your receipt to adult family members. Would they buy your catered lunch?

▶ **Divide to find each quotient.**

1. 2)84   2. 2)62   3. 2)68

4. 3)93   5. 7)70   6. 5)55

7. 3)69   8. 9)99   9. 3)36

10. 9)90   11. 6)66   12. 4)80

Summer is a great time for planting a garden. What would you plant in the garden? To help you decide, ask your family members to vote on what items to plant.

▶ **Follow the directions below to play a fun game of tug-of-war.**

Play tug-of-war. Tie several sturdy pieces of fabric together to make a "rope." Be sure to use a red piece of fabric in the middle. Use a ruler or other straight object to place a line on the ground. Group a few friends or family members into teams. Have each team member get ready at her rope position. Then, have everyone start pulling on the rope at the same time until one team pulls the other across the line. Change the teams. When everyone is done showing her strength, celebrate as a group with refreshing glasses of lemonade.

Go outside with an adult family member on a clear night. Take a look at the surroundings. What do you notice about the trees, shrubs, and buildings? Talk about what you observe.

▶ **Divide to find each quotient.**

1. 6)36   2. 8)40   3. 4)48

4. 7)63   5. 8)56   6. 7)35

7. 9)72   8. 7)28   9. 6)54

10. 5)45   11. 6)24   12. 8)64

Make some signs to serve as a reminder for taking along paper, cloth, or plastic bags on shopping trips. Where will you place the signs so that the next time a family member goes shopping, he brings a reusable bag with him?

▶ **What would you do if you woke up with green hair? Write your answer on the lines below.**

_____
_____
_____
_____
_____
_____
_____
_____
_____
_____
_____

A book publisher has asked you to write a biography. Who is the book about? What is its title? Share your book idea with family members.

▶ **Write the correct homophone from the parentheses to complete each sentence.**

1. Jennifer has two _____ and three oranges.
   (pears, pairs)

2. Brian can never _____ to play the game right.
   (seam, seem)

3. Mother will sift the _____ for the cookies.
   (flour, flower)

4. I hope that I can get everything _____ on time.
   (write, right)

5. Nannette _____ the baking contest.
   (won, one)

6. The bread _____ was very sticky.
   (doe, dough)

Your best friend just got a new bike. You would like one too. You need to convince your family. Write a 30-second commercial about why you should get a new bicycle. Share it with adult family members. Are they ready to buy you a new bike?

▶ **Answer each question about the coordinate grid.**

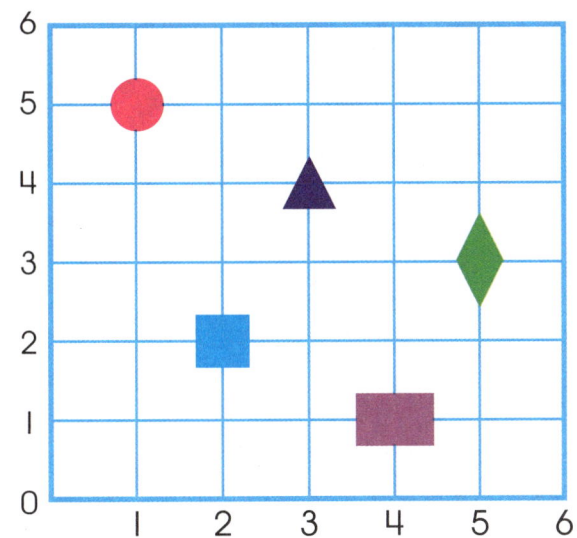

1. Which shape is located at (5, 3)? _____

2. At which coordinate is the square located? _____

3. Circle the shape located at (3, 4).

4. Draw a line to connect the shapes located at (4, 1) and (1, 5).

5. Which shape is located closest to the top? _____

Create the ideal play space for a yard. What is in the play space? Make a three-panel comic strip. Show three special features of the play space. Post your comic strip for family members to see.

▶ **Homophones** are words that sound alike but are spelled differently and have different meanings. Circle the two words in each row that are homophones.

EXAMPLE: tail – tale

1. bear   seen   saw   bare
2. violet   vase   vain   vein
3. drop   dew   down   due
4. tee   tell   told   tea
5. well   weight   wait   went
6. him   hair   hare   held

Make a list of your favorite desserts. Which dessert on the list is especially good during the summer? Talk with an adult family member about the ingredients needed to make this dessert. Perhaps you can add the ingredients to the shopping list.

▶ **Use the clock to answer each question.**

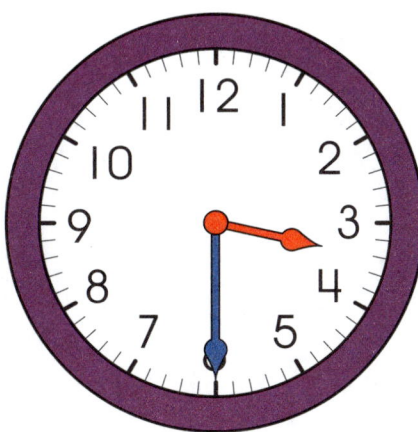

1. What time does the clock show?

   _____

2. How long will it take for the minute hand to move from 6 to 5?

   _____

3. What time will it be when the minute hand reaches 12?

   _____

4. What time will it be when the minute hand moves 15 minutes?

   _____

You are a local weather reporter. You just learned that stormy weather is the forecast for the Fourth of July. You want to keep the viewers happy. How would you do it? Write how you would create a happy Fourth of July weather forecast.

▶ **Write the correct article to complete each sentence.**

1. I enjoyed watching _____ game.

2. Would you like _____ egg salad sandwich?

3. I have _____ dog and _____ cat.

4. Did you hear _____ thunder?

5. An eagle flew over _____ tree.

6. My grandmother gave me _____ new bike.

7. The wind blew my umbrella down _____ street.

8. Mrs. Hayes said that I did _____ good job on my art project.

You just discovered that your dog ate a family member's brand new pair of shoes. Write a note from the dog to the family member. How do you think the dog would apologize?

▶ **Context clues** are the words around a word you do not know. Use context clues to figure out the meaning of each underlined word. Then, circle the letter next to the word's correct meaning.

1. My brother and I often <u>argue</u> about who gets to use the computer.

    A. work   B. disagree   C. study

2. The <u>official</u> told us not to enter the building until 8 o'clock.

    A. person in charge   B. nurse   C. child

3. Josie saw an <u>unusual</u> light in the sky and asked her father what it was.

    A. dark   B. star   C. different

4. The <u>cardinal</u> in my backyard is a beautiful sight. I love his bright red color and sweet song.

    A. singer   B. branch   C. bird with red feathers

5. Mom asked me to turn down the <u>volume</u> on the TV because it was too loud.

    A. noise level   B. book   C. color

Stand with paper and pencil in your room. Count the steps to the front door. Write it down. Next, count the steps to the edge of the street. Write it down. Add the numbers together. How many steps did it take to get from your room to the street?

▶ **Name each figure by its points and label it with the correct symbol.**

EXAMPLES:

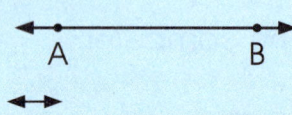
AB = Line AB (or BA)

AB = Line Segment AB (or BA)

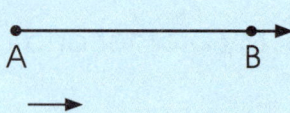
AB = Ray AB

1.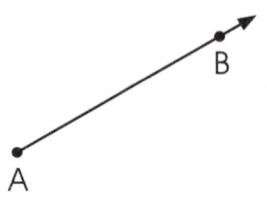

_____

2.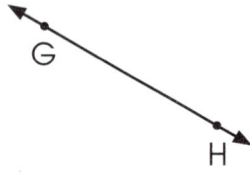

_____

3.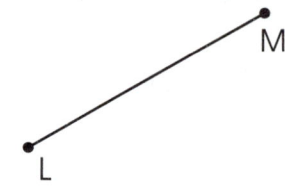

_____

4.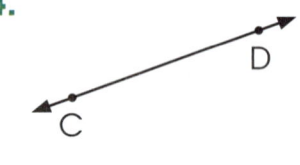

_____

5.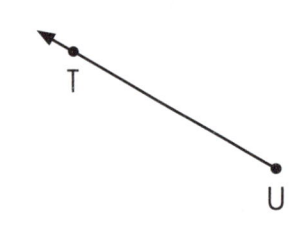

_____

6.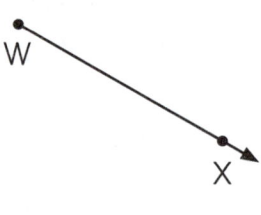

_____

Bake a cake for a family member's birthday. What kind of cake would you make? What would you need to make the cake? How long would it take? Read a cookbook to learn about the process of baking a cake.

▶ An adverb is a word that modifies a verb. Circle the adverb in each sentence. Then, underline the verb that the adverb modifies.

1. On Independence Day, we usually go to the parade.

2. We drive slowly because of traffic.

3. The parade often begins with a marching band.

4. The marching band plays loudly.

5. The huge crowd cheers excitedly.

6. My favorite part is when the big floats pass near us.

7. All of the floats are decorated beautifully.

8. We never see one we don't like.

Ask an adult family member to take you to the grocery store. Take paper and pencil. Make a list of the healthy snack foods you find. Talk about the ones your family would most enjoy.

▶ **Write the correct word from the word bank to complete each sentence.**

| cottage | curtains | bell | pennies |
| quarter | circus | pictures | market |

1. Look at all of the funny _____ in this book.

2. You can buy bread and milk at the _____ .

3. We live in a small _____ .

4. This pencil costs a _____ .

5. I am saving a lot of _____ in a jar.

6. The clowns at the _____ were great.

7. When you hear the _____ , run fast.

8. We have white _____ on our windows.

Make a list of the parks in your town. Which park is the closest to you? Which park is the biggest? Which park is your favorite? Use the Internet to do research on your local parks.

▶ **Write the correct past-tense form of the irregular verb in parentheses to complete each sentence.**

1. Our teacher _____ our class a book about insects. (read)

2. I _____ Mr. Lee before he was my teacher. (know)

3. Ms. Kemp _____ us that we could eat outside today. (tell)

4. Drew _____ that I can borrow his jump rope anytime. (say)

5. I _____ a bird chirping in a tree. (hear)

6. Cody _____ a new baseball glove today. (buy)

7. Hannah _____ her favorite blue shirt under her bed. (find)

8. Brooke and Gene each _____ an apple for a snack. (eat)

Write a story about a day in the life of a pair of shoes. What kind of shoes will you write about? Where will the shoes go during the day? Write the shoe tale and then draw a picture. Share it with your family members.

▶ **Draw a straight line through three numbers that, when added together, total each sum provided.**

1. Sum: 78

20	28	14
16	32	42
19	18	13

2. Sum: 110

16	33	64
39	22	44
51	10	72

3. Sum: 251

71	47	18
82	20	46
98	43	33

4. Sum: 149

15	93	24
63	25	33
63	25	61

5. Sum: 506

94	100	90
88	206	58
79	200	96

6. Sum: 189

94	100	90
88	20	58
79	10	96

You are the news reporter for your family's nightly news. Make a list of 10 questions to ask family members that will help you write a news report about your family's dog. Share your questions with adult family members. What are their answers?

▶ **Write the correct past- or present-tense form of the verb in parentheses to complete each sentence.**

1. My friends and I like to _____ clay animals. (make)

2. Yesterday, we _____ the clay into different shapes. (roll)

3. Jeremy _____ making a clay hippo yesterday. (enjoy)

4. Our teacher _____ us bake the clay animals. (help)

5. He always _____ them in the kiln. (place)

6. After they were baked and cooled, we _____ them. (paint)

7. Often, we _____ them as gifts. (give)

Go on a number search in your neighborhood. Write at least 10 numbers you see. Pick two of the numbers to add. Pick two numbers and subtract. Pick two numbers and multiply. Show your math problems to adult family members. Do they get the same answers?

▶ One word has been highlighted in each sentence below. There are two definitions given for the word. Decide which meaning is correct by reading the sentence and thinking about how the word is used. Circle the correct meaning.

EXAMPLE:

The **bail** was broken, so the bucket of water was difficult to lift.

A. throw water out   B. (the handle of a pail)

1. The princess had a grand time at the **ball** last night.

   A. a dance   B. a round object

2. Joe **left** before I could tell him good-bye.

   A. the opposite of right   B. went away

3. Jack had a **fit** when his brother broke his new bicycle.

   A. suitable   B. a tantrum

4. The group became **grave** when they saw the danger they were in.

   A. serious   B. a place of burial

You are attending chef school. Your assignment for the day is to bake the most delicious bread. What kind of bread would you make? What ingredients would you need? Talk with an adult family member about the bread assignment. Might the adult family member help you make the bread?

▶ Read each group of words. Write the words in the correct order to make complete sentences. Use correct punctuation and capitalization.

1. rode hill the I down on bike a _____

_____

2. garden a our mom backyard I planted and in my _____

_____

3. themselves elephant animals when braced all the sneezed the of _____

_____

4. bottles of full wagon a pulled cory _____

_____

5. book went I bed closed and my to _____

_____

Time to play school. You are the teacher, and your first job is to make an assignment for the day. What is it? Share your assignment with friends. Are they willing to do it?

▶ **Continue each counting pattern.**

1. 0   3   6   9   12   ___   ___   ___   24   ___

2. 6   12   18   24   ___   ___   48   ___   ___

3. 12   16   20   24   ___   ___   ___   44   ___

4. 33   30   27   24   ___   ___   ___   9   ___

5. 100   98   96   94   ___   ___   86   ___   ___

You have just been named captain of a team. What kind of team is it? What is the team's name? What are the team's colors? Use paper and markers to draw a picture of yourself in the team uniform. Post your picture for family members to see.

▶ **Read the passage. Then, answer the questions.**

Silkworms

Silk is a soft, smooth type of cloth that is used for clothing, bedding, and wall hangings. It comes from silkworm cocoons, which are spun into thread that is then made into cloth. It takes about 3,000 cocoons to make one pound (about 0.5 kg) of silk. Silkworms become moths as adults. Like most insects, silkworms go through four stages. The moth lays its eggs on a mulberry leaf. After a silkworm hatches into a caterpillar, it munches on leaves until it grows to the length of a human finger. After about a month of eating and growing, the worm spins a cocoon of silk around itself. Spinning the cocoon takes about three days. Inside the cocoon, the silkworm changes shape and becomes a pupa. After about three weeks, the pupa turns into a moth. The moth comes out of the cocoon and starts the cycle all over again.

1. What is the main idea of this passage?
    A. Silkworm cocoons are spun into thread.
    B. Silkworms turn into moths as adults
    C. Silkworms go through four stages and help make silk.

2. What is silk used for? _____
   _____

3. What are the stages of a silkworm's life? _____
   _____

4. How long does it take to spin a cocoon?
    A. 31,000 days   B. about three days   C. about three weeks

When you were a young child, what was your favorite toy? Draw a picture of it and then write a poem about yourself and the toy. Share your poem with family members. Do they remember your favorite toy too?

▶ **Temperatures are measured in degrees Fahrenheit (°F) and degrees Celsius (°C).** Thirty-two degrees Fahrenheit is equal to 0 degrees Celsius. Write the temperature shown on each thermometer.

1. _____ °F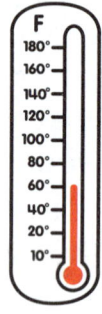

2. _____ °F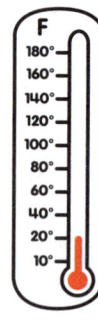

3. _____ °F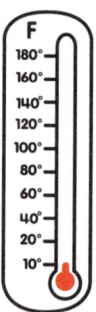

4. _____ °C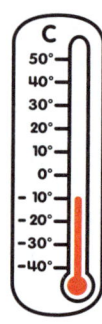

5. _____ °C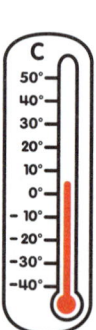

6. _____ °C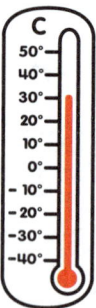

Practice pantomiming the steps for washing your hands: Wet your hands with running water. Apply soap. Lather well. Rub your hands for 20 seconds. Rinse well. Dry your hands. Share your pantomime with family members and friends.

▶ **Read the story. Then, answer the questions.**

The Broken Window

The children were playing baseball in the empty lot. Peggy was at bat. She swung hard and hit the ball farther than anyone else had. The ball sailed across the lot and smashed through Mrs. Allen's window. Peggy knew Mrs. Allen would be really angry. The other kids scattered, running for home. Peggy looked at the broken window.

1. What do you think Peggy will do?

   _____
   _____
   _____
   _____

2. Which clues helped you to decide?

   _____
   _____
   _____
   _____

Begin an exercise program. Make a list of at least three exercises. Then, do them. When you are done, write about how you feel. Share your writing with family members. Are they ready to exercise with you?

▶ Each side of a geometric solid is called a face. Write the number of faces for each solid.

1.

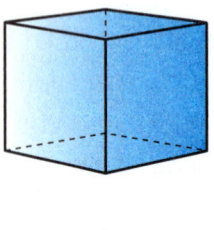

cube

 faces

2.

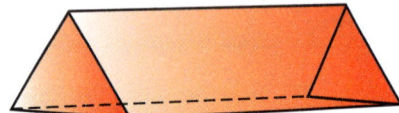

triangular prism

 faces

_____ faces

3.

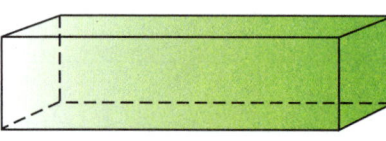

rectangular prism

 faces

_____ faces

Put your hands together and clap, clap, clap. How many different clapping rhythms can you make? Share your clapping rhythms with family and friends. Invite them to clap along with you.

▶ An outcome is the result of an event. Decide whether the following outcomes are certain (will definitely happen), possible (might happen), or impossible (will not happen). Write your answer on the line.

1. It will rain tomorrow. _____

2. You will grow to be 50 feet tall. _____

3. The Vikings will win the Super Bowl next season. _____

4. Tomorrow will be 24 hours long. _____

5. Humans will travel to Mars. _____

6. New Year's Eve will fall on December 31. _____

Have you been sitting around too much? Well, it is time to move around and make up a dance. Put on some music and create some steps. Then, teach your dance to your friends.

▶ **Divide to find each quotient.**

1. $3\overline{)24}$ 2. $7\overline{)56}$ 3. $7\overline{)49}$

4. $5\overline{)5}$ 5. $9\overline{)45}$ 6. $4\overline{)36}$

7. $9\overline{)36}$ 8. $5\overline{)35}$ 9. $9\overline{)27}$

10. $8\overline{)32}$ 11. $6\overline{)66}$ 12. $8\overline{)16}$

Take a pencil and a notebook and sit in your favorite chair. Imagine the chair can talk. Write a letter from the chair to you. What words of advice does the chair have for you? Share the letter with family members.

▶ **Follow the directions below to learn the "up-down."**

There are many great exercises to improve your strength. One that uses your entire body is called an up-down. Begin by running in place. Then, drop to the ground with your chest to the floor and your legs straight behind you. Do one push-up. Then, jump back to your feet and run in place again. Remember to start slowly. Although it is not easy, doing up-downs is a great way to improve your overall fitness.

Go outside with paper, a pencil, and a jump rope. Find a good place for jumping rope. Keep track of how many times you jump before you miss. Write the number on the paper. Continue jumping rope until you miss again. Write down the number and add the two numbers. Can you keep jumping until you reach 100 jumps?

▶ **Answer each question.**

1. How many 6s are in 18? _____

2. How many 9s are in 18? _____

3. How many 5s are in 25? _____

4. How many 7s are in 21? _____

5. How many 2s are in 8? _____

6. How many 8s are in 32? _____

7. How many 4s are in 20? _____

8. How many 6s are in 36? _____

You feel your family needs an exercise program. You decide that walking would be the best group exercise. Create a poster that promotes a family walking program. Post it for your family members to see. Are they ready to walk with you?

▶ Read each sentence. If the underlined word is spelled correctly, write *correct*. If it is spelled incorrectly, rewrite the word with the correct spelling.

1. I'd like a glass of water. _____

2. Do you know where they've been today? _____

3. Be carefull with that knife. _____

4. My mom was very unhappy today. _____

5. What did Joni plant in her gardin? _____

6. We looked at all of the babyies in the hospital. _____

7. Aunt Mary canned 10 pounds of cherries. _____

8. He waved at us from the window. _____

9. Did you like the new movee? _____

10. Remember to set your alarm clock. _____

How many places are there in your home where family members can wash their hands? Make reminder signs for washing hands. Then, post one at each hand-washing spot. Let your family know the signs are there to help them stay healthy.

▶ **Read the story. Then, answer the questions.**

Good Friends

Robert and Kaye are two of my best friends. We have gone to school together since we were in kindergarten. We even go to summer camp and the recreation center together. There are many reasons why I like to spend time with them. Robert always lets me borrow his skateboard. He knows that if I had a skateboard, I would let him borrow it. Robert is a person I can count on too. When we are out riding our bikes together, Kaye sometimes lets me ride in front while she rides behind me. She understands that one way to be a good friend is by taking turns and being fair.

1. How is Robert a good friend? _____
   _____
   _____

2. Is Kaye a fair person? Why? _____
   _____
   _____

3. List three things that the friends do together. _____
   _____
   _____

What jump rope chants do you know? Do you have a favorite one? Take paper and a pencil and write a rhythmic jump rope chant. Then, share it with a friend.

▶ **Solve each word problem. Show your work.**

1. Nancy's dog weighs 63 pounds. Janet's dog weighs 54 pounds. How many pounds do the two dogs weigh altogether?

2. Jake collected 694 marbles. Joyce collected 966. How many fewer marbles did Jake collect than Joyce?

3. Reid threw 259 balls. Kirk threw 137 balls. How many more balls did Reid throw than Kirk?

4. Sasha has 42 cards. She divides them into 6 equal stacks. How many cards are in each stack?

You are a sports reporter. Interview family members and ask them about their favorite sports teams. Then, write a report about what you learn. Present your report to family members as if you are a TV reporter.

▶ **Read each pair of words. For each pair, write one way the two things are alike and one way they are different.**

1. leopard, cheetah _____

   _____

   _____

2. keyboard, piano _____

   _____

   _____

3. cabin, tent _____

   _____

   _____

4. whistle, sing _____

   _____

   _____

Do you like amusement parks? Do you have a favorite ride? Make a list of amusement park rides. Show a friend the list. Does your friend have any rides to add to the list? Would you be willing to go on all of the rides?

▶ Write the missing form of each irregular verb. Use a dictionary if needed.

Present	Past	Past with *has* or *have*
1. sing		has or have sung
2. tell	told	has or have
3. bring		has or have brought
4. wear	wore	has or have
5. take		has or have taken

You are a comedian. Write a joke for your family's dinner tonight. Present the joke to your family. Do they laugh? If not, do they have a better joke?

▶ **Read the following word problems. Make notes to help you find the order of the people in each problem. Circle the correct answer.**

1. Four marathon runners ran in a race. Use the clues to determine the winner.

   > Mario ran faster than Shane.
   > Shane ran faster than Randy.
   > Tyler ran faster than Mario.

   Who won the race?

   A. Mario

   B. Randy

   C. Shane

   D. Tyler

2. Davis lined up his four sisters by height. Use the clues below to determine the order of the sisters.

   > Sally is taller than Kendra.
   > Mary is the tallest sister.
   > Trisha is not as tall as Kendra.

   In what order did the sisters stand?

   A. Mary, Trisha, Kendra, Sally

   B. Mary, Sally, Trisha, Kendra

   C. Mary, Sally, Kendra, Trisha

   D. Sally, Mary, Trisha, Kendra

Write a note to a family member. Use words you find in old magazines. Look through the magazines and cut out words. Then, share your message with your family member.

▶ **Write the plural form of the underlined word to complete each sentence.**

1. The <u>wolf</u> howled until two more _____ howled with him.

2. She put that book on the top <u>shelf</u> and all of the other books on the bottom _____ .

3. The horse has a special horseshoe on its chipped <u>hoof</u> and regular horseshoes on its other _____ .

4. The <u>child</u> played alone until the other _____ came.

5. His <u>wife</u> talked with some other _____ at the meeting.

6. Did you see the yellow <u>leaf</u> in that pile of _____ ?

Write a report on the different kinds of jobs your neighbors have. Make a two-column chart. Have an adult family member work with you. In one column, make a list of the neighbors you know. In the second column, identify their jobs. What did you learn about your neighbors?

▶ **Use the words from the word bank to solve the crossword puzzle.**

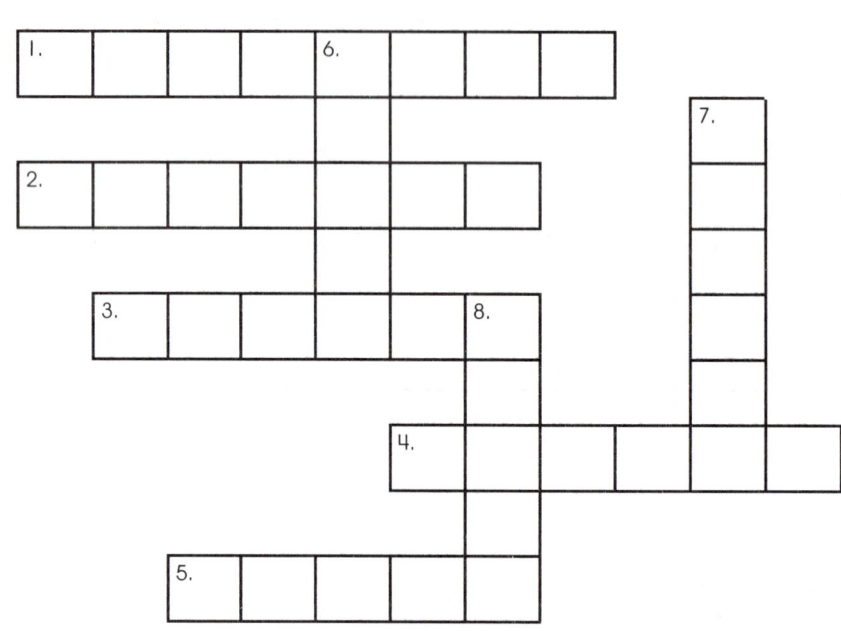

Across
1. very sure
2. to make something look larger
3. to go behind
4. needs to be done now
5. to care for the sick

Down
6. to spin
7. to send back
8. not better

Take a look in your kitchen. Make a list of fruits you find. Keep track of the fruits you eat through the day. Share your list with an adult family member. Are there any fruits you would like to have eaten, but did not?

▶ **Add the correct ending (*s* or *es*) to make each word plural. Write the new words on the lines.**

1. teacher _____
2. potato _____
3. house _____
4. kite _____
5. class _____
6. clown _____
7. box _____
8. handbook _____
9. watch _____
10. friend _____
11. clock _____
12. computer _____
13. couch _____
14. caramel _____

Time to go on a home safari! Search for clocks around your home. List the clocks you find. Note the room where they are located. Then, review your list. Which clock is the biggest? Which clock is the smallest? Share your list with family members.

▶ Write the letter of each definition next to the correct geometry term.

1. _____ parallel lines

2. _____ perpendicular lines

3. _____ vertex

4. _____ face

5. _____ edge

6. _____ ray

7. _____ line segment

8. _____ angle

9. _____ intersecting lines

A. a line with one endpoint that continues in one direction

B. the endpoint of three line segments on a solid figure

C. a flat surface of a solid figure

D. where two or more faces of a solid figure meet

E. lines that intersect to form four right angles

F. the space between two nonparallel rays that share an endpoint

G. lines that cross at only one point

H. a line with two endpoints

I. lines that never intersect

You just won a contest and the prize is a new car! You can have any car you want. Look through old magazines. Cut out pictures of cars you like. Show the cars to family members. Take a poll to see which car your family prefers.

▶ **Read each sentence below. Circle the homonym that completes each sentence correctly.**

1. While in the woods, Kristen saw a (bear   bare).

2. Candy fell and hurt her (tow   toe).

3. The (sale   sail) on the boat billowed in the wind.

4. Sherry did not feel well and looked (pail   pale).

5. Teddy does not (know   no) how to play basketball.

6. We went to the mailbox and (cent   sent) a letter.

7. My cat had six kittens and four of them are (mail   male).

8. Sissy stopped to pick a (flour   flower) from the garden.

Help young children learn about community helpers. Make a list of five types of jobs that serve the community. Then, make a five-panel comic strip showing how each job serves the community. Share your comic strip with family and friends.

▶ **Read the story. Then, answer the questions.**

Pink Sunglasses

Tara found a pair of pink sunglasses on the bus. They had red lightning bolts on the earpieces. Tara liked them. After lunch, she put on the sunglasses to wear at recess. A girl ran to her and said, "Excuse me, but I think those are mine." Tara's heart sank.

1. What do you think Tara will do? _____

   _____

   _____

   _____

2. Which clues helped you decide? _____

   _____

   _____

   _____

Start a fitness club for your friends. Create a 30-second commercial for the fitness club. Share it with your friends. Are they ready to join the club?

▶ **Make each highlighted word possessive by rewriting the word on the line and adding an apostrophe in the correct place.**

1. That is **Danas** dollhouse. _____

2. **Craigs** truck is very big. _____

3. I like **Sharons** new green bicycle. _____

4. The **childrens** song was perfectly in tune. _____

5. The two **girls** kites flew high in the sky. _____

6. The **schools** end-of-the-year picnic was fun. _____

7. The **trucks** loud horn scared Barbara. _____

8. The **actors** costume was colorful. _____

9. I love to visit my **grandmothers** house. _____

10. The **singers** voices are beautiful. _____

11. Those **dogs** collars are green. _____

Time on your hands? Look through some old catalogs. Pick a watch for each family member. Cut out the picture of the watch. Write its price on paper. Once you have selected a watch for each family member, add to find the total cost. Share the results with an adult family member.

▶ Use the words from the word bank to solve the crossword puzzle.

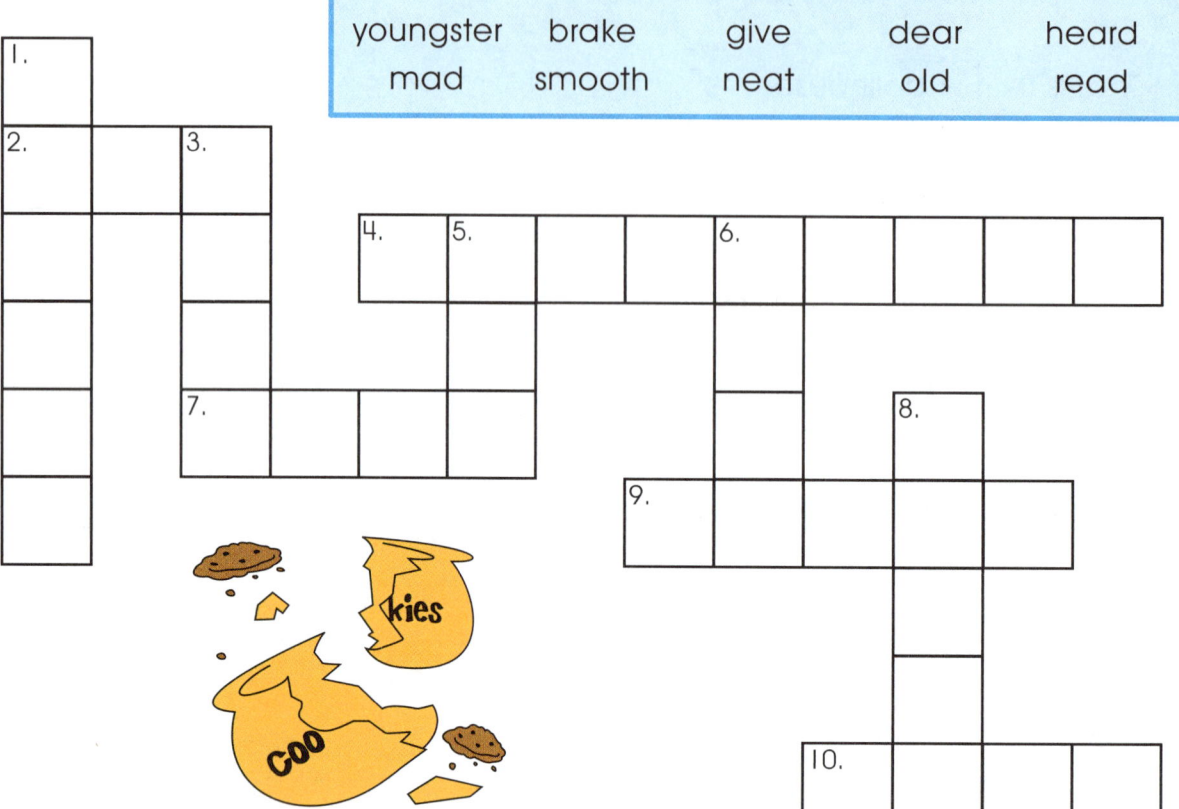

youngster brake give dear heard
mad smooth neat old read

Across

2. A synonym for angry
4. A synonym for child
7. A homophone for red
9. A homophone for herd
10. A synonym for tidy

Down

1. An antonym for rough
3. A homophone for deer
5. An antonym for new
6. An antonym for take
8. A homophone for break

You are a pet costume designer. Make a four-panel comic strip showing your four best pet costume designs. Share your designs with family members and friends. Do they have a favorite design?

▶ Write **right**, **straight**, **acute**, or **obtuse** to identify each angle.

Right Angle: 90° angle	Straight Angle: 180° angle
Acute Angle: Measures less than 90°	Obtuse Angle: Measures more than 90° but less than 180°

1. 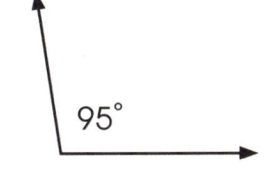 95°

   _____

2. 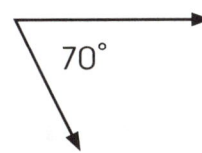 70°

   _____

3. 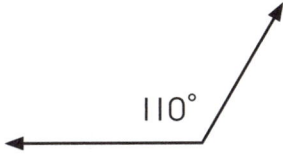 110°

   _____

4. 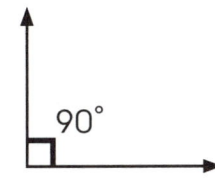 90°

   _____

Make a list of questions to ask friends and family members about their favorite foods. Make a bar graph to display your results.

▶ **Write the contraction for each pair of words.**

1. we are _____

2. were not _____

3. was not _____

4. would not _____

▶ **Write the pair of words that makes each contraction.**

5. they've _____

6. they'll _____

7. shouldn't _____

8. I'd _____

Make a family tree. Find a branch with many limbs. Write the names of your family members on pieces of paper. Tie each name to a limb to represent that person's place in your family.

▶ Read each clue. Write the missing vowels to complete each word.

1. a sea animal with eight legs   ___ct___p___s

2. a reptile that lives in a swamp   cr___c___d___l___

3. a very small house   c___tt___g___

4. something to keep the rain off   ___mbr___ll___

5. something that is completely different   ___pp___s___t___

6. a place that has little rain   d___s___rt

Find a box of tissues. Hold it in your hand. Look around the room. Make a tally mark for each thing you see that would fit inside the box. How many things do you see? Then, try it again in another room.

▶ **Read the directions from the oatmeal box. Then, answer the questions.**

> **Instant Oatmeal**
> 1. Empty the package into a microwave-safe bowl.
> 2. Add ⅔ cup (156 mL) water and stir.
> 3. Microwave on high for 1 to 2 minutes; stir.
> 4. Pour some milk on top if desired.
> 5. Let cool; eat with a spoon.

1. What do the directions tell you how to make?

   A. oatmeal
   B. instant oatmeal
   C. cold cereal

2. What is the first step? _____

3. What materials do you need? _____

   _____

4. How long should it take to make this?

   A. a few seconds
   B. a few minutes
   C. 30 minutes

Design a float for a Fourth of July parade. Use a box to build a small model of the float. Share the finished model with your family.

▶ **Write the prefix re- or un- in each blank to complete the sentences.**

1. Please _____ move your shoes before you come in.

2. That was an _____ usual movie.

3. I would like to _____ new the magazine subscription.

4. That was an _____ common rainstorm.

5. You will have to _____ tell the story later.

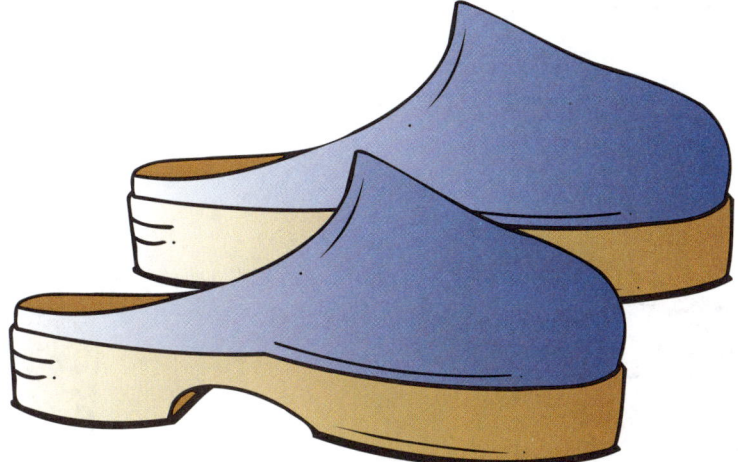

You have hundreds of dishes to wash by hand. You decide that music might help you get the dish-washing beat. What kind of music will you play? Make a list of five songs. Share your list with a family member and ask her to help you add more songs.

▶ **Underline the spelling error in each sentence. Write the correct spelling of the word on the line.**

1. Are you goeing to the ball game? _____

2. My room is very cleen. _____

3. Ronnie baught some gum at the store. _____

4. Tony payed $15.00 to get his bike fixed. _____

5. Pepper makes Becky sneaze. _____

6. Billy loves ice creem. _____

7. Travis is very frendly. _____

Play a game of echo clapping. Have a family member or friend play the game with you. One person claps a rhythm. The second person responds with the same rhythmic clapping pattern. Take turns going first. The clapping can go on and on.

▶ **Write a sentence for each word in the word bank.**

| hooves | lives | leaves | scarves | shelves |

1. _____

2. _____

3. _____

4. _____

5. _____

Stand in your kitchen and look around. Look for things that need to be plugged in to work. Make a list of what you discover. Then, go to another room and add to the list. How many things did you find altogether?

▶ **Circle the pronoun that completes each sentence.**

1. _____ grew corn and tomatoes in his garden.

    Him   His   He

2. Please tell _____ what vegetables you would like to plant this year.

    we   mine   us

3. Tisha and _____ love to plant our watermelon seeds.

    we   I   us

4. Mother wants to plant flowers in her garden so that _____ will have something special.

    us   mine   she

5. We plant carrots, lettuce, and beans because _____ are good to eat.

    they   them   she

You would like a cat. Use paper and markers to draw a picture of a cat. Then, give the cat a name. Share your picture with your family. How do they like the new cat's name?

▶ **Study the table of contents. Then, answer the questions.**

Table of Contents
Communicating with Others 9
Writing a Story................................16
Word Meanings..............................20
Following Directions......................25
Using Words Correctly 32
Commas..40
Proofreading..................................53
Describing Words 57

1. What chapter should you read to learn about writing a story?

   _____

2. On what page should you start reading to learn about commas?

   _____

3. On what page should you start reading to learn how to describe what

   something looks like? _____

The weather is hot. A summertime drink will help you cool off. Make a list of ingredients you need to make the drink. Then, share the list with an adult family member. Can he help you make the drink?

▶ **Write the correct word from the word bank on each line to complete the story.**

| classroom | backpack | breakfast | playground | homework |

My School Day

My stepfather wakes me up to get dressed and eat _____.

I pack my _____ and go to school. I work at my desk in

the _____. At recess, my friends and I go to the

_____. At the end of the day, our teacher

writes our _____ assignment on the board.

You just won a trip for your family! Where would you want to go? Would you choose a theme park, a beach, a national park, or some other country to visit? Ask your family members where they would want to go. Share the results with your family.

▶ **Solve each word problem. Show your work.**

1. Thad planted 5 seeds in each of 9 holes. How many seeds did he plant?

2. Mia has the same number of nickels as she has dimes. She has $1.80 worth of dimes. How many nickels does she have?

3. Jill babysat 4 times last week. She made $4 one night, $5.25 on two different nights, and $6.40 on another night. How much did Jill make altogether?

4. There were 95 children on the bus. Then, 12 got off at the first stop. Twenty-two got off at the second stop. How many children were left on the bus?

Promote fire safety in your home. Make a three-panel comic strip about home fire safety. Then, post your comic strip for family members to view.

▶ **For each question below, decide which part of the word is underlined. Write** *base word*, *prefix*, or *suffix* **on the line.**

1. punish<u>ment</u> _____
2. dark<u>ness</u> _____
3. <u>dis</u>appear _____
4. <u>pre</u>cook _____
5. pre<u>soak</u> _____
6. proud<u>ly</u> _____
7. place<u>ment</u> _____
8. <u>dis</u>trust _____
9. color<u>less</u> _____
10. friend<u>ly</u> _____
11. <u>sick</u>ness _____
12. <u>sugar</u>less _____
13. fool<u>ish</u> _____
14. brown<u>ish</u> _____
15. <u>re</u>fill _____
16. re<u>pay</u> _____
17. <u>un</u>sure _____
18. lone<u>ly</u> _____

Write a story about a day in the life of two animals. What are the animals' names? Where do they live? What will they do in the story? Write the story and then draw a picture to illustrate it.

▶ **Read the story. Then, write an ending to the story.**

Missing in the Museum

The three friends had not seen Logan for a long time. They were standing in the main room of the natural history museum. "He was here a little while ago," said Kim. The museum was closing. Most of the other visitors had already left.

"Logan likes the dinosaur exhibit and the astronomy room," said Craig. "Maybe we should go look there."

Just then, a museum guard said, "Sorry, but the museum is closing. You'll have to come back tomorrow."

_____

_____

_____

_____

_____

_____

_____

_____

Interview a member of your favorite sports team. Make a list of 10 questions for the interview. Share the interview questions with a family member. Talk about the questions and add other questions to the list.

▶ **Answer each question about the coordinate grid.**

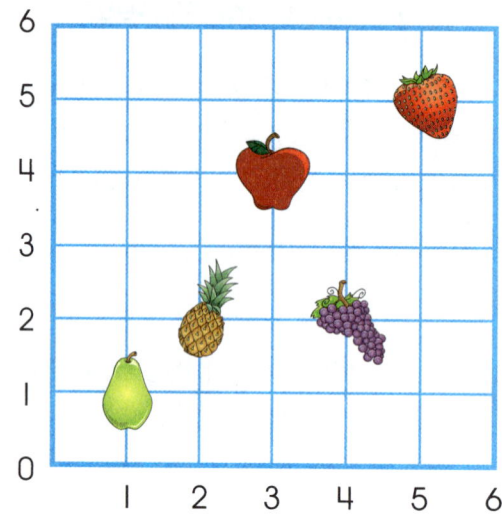

1. Which fruit is located at (3, 4)? _____

2. Which fruit is located at (5, 5)? _____

3. At which coordinate is the pear located? _____

4. Draw a square around the fruit located at (4, 2).

5. Circle the fruit located at (2, 2).

6. Draw a peach at (5, 3).

Be a disc jockey for an upcoming family party. You need to create a list of music. Talk with family members about possible music to play. Then, make a list of what you will play. Share the list with family members.

▶ A **simile** compares two unlike things using the words *like* or *as*. Complete each sentence by making a comparison.

EXAMPLE:

The daffodils were as yellow as _____*lemons*_____.

1. The piano keys were as white as _____.

2. The fireworks were as bright as the _____.

3. His eyes were as green as the _____.

4. The balloons were like a bunch of _____.

5. Her eyes sparkled like _____.

6. The wind was as gentle as _____.

Take a family member with you on a number quest. Together, look through a magazine. Talk about the numbers you see and how the numbers are used.

▶ **Count the money in each box. Write the total for each group on the line.**

1.

$_____ . _____

2.

$_____ . _____

3.

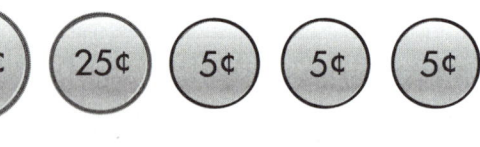

$_____ . _____

4.

$_____ . _____

Promote conserving water in your home. Make a three-panel comic strip showing three ways for your family to save water. Then, post your comic strip for family members to see.

▶ The **main idea** tells what a story is about. Underline the sentence in each story that tells the main idea.

1. Penny's dog Coco likes to eat special snacks. Coco eats carrots. She also likes cheese. Her favorite snack is peanut butter dog biscuits. Penny makes sure that Coco does not eat too many snacks. They also go for a walk every afternoon.

2. Oliver Owl is teaching Owen Owl to fly. Oliver tells Owen to perch on the highest branch of the tallest tree. "Then, jump and flap your wings as hard as you can," he says. Owen is nervous, but he trusts Oliver. He jumps from the branch and flaps his wings. Oliver cheers as Owen starts to fly! Later, Owen says that Oliver is good at teaching little owls how to fly.

Find a reusable shopping bag. Imagine that the bag could tell you what it thought. Use a pencil and paper to write a note from the shopping bag to your family. Let your family know how much the bag likes to go grocery shopping with them. Share the letter with family members.

▶ Use the rules in the box to help you answer each question. Write *yes* or *no* on the line provided.

RULES:
1 centimeter (cm) = 10 millimeters (mm)
1 decimeter (dm) = 10 centimeters
1 meter (m) = 100 centimeters
1 kilometer (km) = 1,000 meters

EXAMPLE:
Is 1 m longer than 120 cm?
1 m = 100 cm, so 1 meter is not longer than 120 cm.
ANSWER: *no*

1. Is 15 cm longer than 1 dm? _____
2. Is 5 dm longer than 1 m? _____
3. Is 900 m longer than 1 km? _____
4. Is 1 m longer than 90 cm? _____
5. Is 1 m longer than 1 dm? _____
6. Is 20 cm longer than 1 m? _____
7. Is 5 mm longer than 1 cm? _____
8. Is 2 km longer than 1,500 m? _____
9. Is 2 cm longer than 10 mm? _____
10. Is 15 dm longer than 1 m? _____

Stand in your kitchen and look at a clock. What time is it? Write the time on a sheet of paper. Then, write what time it will be in 30 minutes and in 90 minutes.

▶ **Follow the directions below to build your self-discipline.**

Self-discipline means making yourself do what you know you should. Showing self-discipline can be difficult. But, it becomes easier with practice.

Read the following situation. On a separate sheet of paper, write the possible consequence of not using self-discipline. Then, write the reward for showing self-discipline.

You have been learning to play guitar, and you have become pretty good. During the school year, you practiced for at least 20 minutes every day. Your lessons start again in August. Sometimes, other activities pop up during the summer, such as swimming practice and other fun outdoor activities. Playing guitar every day can seem like a chore when there are other cool things to do.

A family member just gave you $40.00. You decide to do some catalog shopping. Look through a catalog. Make a list of three things you could buy with the $40.00. How many different sets of these items could you buy?

▶ **What is the funniest thing your grandparents or other relatives have told you about another family member? Retell the story.**

_____
_____
_____
_____
_____
_____
_____
_____
_____
_____
_____
_____

Go for an animal observation walk around your neighborhood. Take a pencil and a notebook with you. Write the different animals you see. Rank the animals from largest to smallest. Which animal was your favorite?

American Education Publishing™

▶ **Write the correct unit of measurement to complete each sentence.**

| 1 meter (m) = 100 centimeters (cm)   1 kilometer (km) = 1,000 meters (m) |

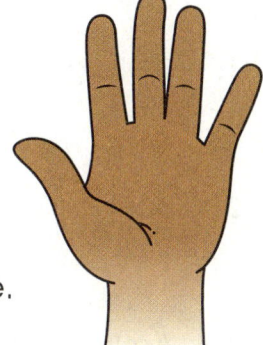

1. Reid is 150 _____ tall.

2. Paige's room is 5 _____ wide.

3. Whitney's hand is 14 _____ long and 5 _____ wide.

4. Mr. Suarez drove his car 84 _____ the first hour.

5. The distance from Chicago, Illinois, to Denver, Colorado, is 1,466 _____ .

6. Myla's kitchen is approximately 7 _____ wide.

7. The flagpole at the post office is 46 _____ tall.

8. Lin and Tara walked approximately 3 _____ in 30 minutes.

Create your own game! Decide if the game will be played indoors or outdoors. Make up the rules for the game. Share the game idea with family and friends. Are they ready to play?

▶ A pronoun is a word that takes the place of a noun. Read each sentence and circle the noun(s) that each underlined pronoun is replacing.

EXAMPLE:

Betty has a (computer). She keeps <u>it</u> on her desk.

1. Liv forgot her umbrella. She went home to get <u>it</u>.

2. Benji asked Juan if <u>he</u> was going to play baseball this year.

3. Amira and Becca both collect seashells. Sometimes, <u>they</u> trade with each other.

4. Rachel plays the violin, and sometimes <u>she</u> sings too.

5. We gave our dog a new toy. Fido barked when he saw <u>it</u>.

6. Our school bus is always crowded, and <u>it</u> is usually noisy too.

Start a pet fitness club. Create a 30-second commercial for the club. Promote how the club will benefit both the owners and their dogs and cats. Share your commercial with your friends.

▶ **Area** is the space inside a figure. It is measured in square units. You can find the area by counting the number of squares in the figure. Look at the following figures and find the area of each.

1.

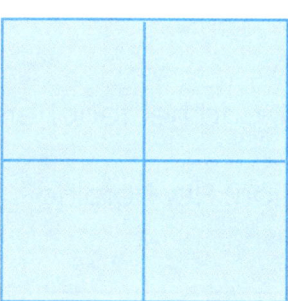

Area = _____ square units

2.

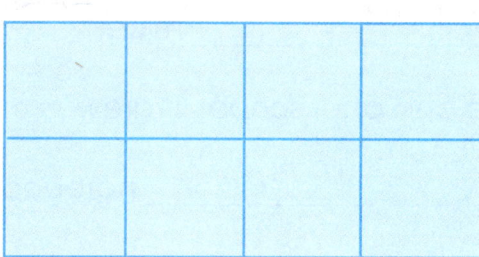

Area = _____ square units

Promote fire safety in your neighborhood. Write a letter to your neighbors about how they can protect themselves from fires in their homes. Use the Internet to help research fire prevention tips.

▶ An **adjective** is a word that describes something. Read the story below. Some of the adjectives are missing. Fill in the blanks using words from the word bank.

best	dark	great	longer	tiny
brilliant	deep	green	slender	vast
creative	famous	long	tall	whole

The Author

Angelica decided to write a book. She loved to read, and her teachers said that she had a _____ imagination. Her heroine would have _____ eyes and _____, _____ hair, just like Angelica. She would live in the middle of a _____, _____ forest. Angelica imagined the animals that might come to visit her character: _____ bears, _____ deer, and _____ mice. She worked on her story every day at lunchtime and after school. It grew _____ and soon took up a _____ notebook! Angelica let her _____ friend, Isabel, read her story. Isabel thought it was _____ and very _____. She said she could not wait until Angelica was a _____ author one day!

Go to a window in your home that gives you a good view of the outdoors. Take paper and a pencil with you. Make a list of what you see that is the color red. How many red things do you see?

▶ **Find the area of each figure.**

1.

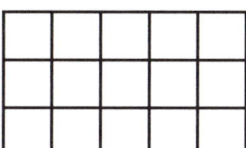

_____ × _____ = _____
 base   height   total area

2.

_____ × _____ = _____
 base   height   total area

3.

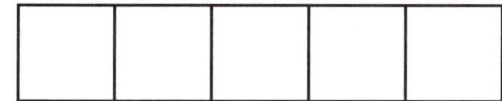

_____ × _____ = _____
 base   height   total area

4.

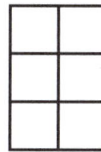

_____ × _____ = _____
 base   height   total area

Find a ball that has a good bounce to it. Take the ball and a timer and go outside. Bounce the ball. Count the number of bounces. How many bounces in a minute? Five minutes?

▶ **Read each group of related words. Write two more related words for each group.**

EXAMPLE:

robin, owl, pigeon   _duck_   _hawk_

1. peaches, apples, pears   _____   _____

2. spoon, bowl, cup   _____   _____

3. lake, pond, river   _____   _____

4. branches, sticks, wood   _____   _____

5. lemonade, water, milk   _____   _____

6. dollar, dime, penny   _____   _____

7. carrot, celery, cucumber _____   _____

8. dress, shoes, skirt   _____   _____

9. tennis, golf, racquetball _____   _____

Have an adult family member sit with you. Talk about the different kinds of jobs in a hospital. Together, make a list of hospital workers. Count the different jobs on your list. How many do you have altogether?

▶ **Write the missing factors.**

1. ____ × 3 = 6
2. ____ × 6 = 30
3. 4 × ____ = 16
4. 3 × ____ = 18
5. 7 × ____ = 14
6. ____ × 9 = 18
7. ____ × 5 = 5
8. 12 × ____ = 12
9. ____ × 8 = 24
10. 1 × ____ = 9
11. 4 × ____ = 28
12. 9 × ____ = 81
13. 3 × ____ = 21
14. ____ × 5 = 25
15. ____ × 7 = 49
16. ____ × 2 = 4
17. 4 × ____ = 24
18. ____ × 8 = 64

Jumping rope is good exercise. Ask a friend or family member to jump rope with you. Take turns jumping. Keep track of how many times each one of you jumps without a miss. Who is able to jump more times without a miss?

▶ **Write the correct word from the word bank on each line to complete the passage.**

| plant | heat | sunlight | Earth | oxygen | plants |

Sunlight is very important to our planet, _____.

Most of our food comes from _____ life.

_____ also give off the _____ we

breathe. Without _____, plants would die, and we

would not have food or air. The _____ of the sun also

warms Earth. Without it, we would freeze.

Your job today is to listen for your name. Take paper and a pencil. Make a tally mark every time you hear your name used. At the end of the day, count the tally marks. Share the results with your family.

▶ **Solve each word problem. Show your work and write the answers in the space provided.**

1. Sophia's Bakery sold 8 cakes each day for 21 days. How many cakes did the bakery sell in all?

2. Regina made 49 gift baskets each week for 5 weeks. Estimate how many gift baskets she made.

3. For 21 days of camp, Melanie collected 2 souvenirs each day. How many souvenirs did she collect in all?

4. Donna sold 136 bags of popcorn at the movie theater each day for 24 days. Estimate to find out about how many bags of popcorn Donna sold.

Be a designer. Use paper and markers to create a name plaque for the door to your room. Share your finished design with family members.

▶ Write a synonym from the word bank for each word.

alter	error	connect	afraid	jewel
~~simple~~	cent	present	finish	sofa

EXAMPLE:

easy ____simple____

1. mistake _____

2. scared _____

3. couch _____

4. gift _____

5. join _____

6. complete _____

7. gem _____

8. penny _____

9. change _____

What is your favorite color? Make a list of foods that are your favorite color. Create a menu for a meal serving foods that are your favorite color. Share your menu with family members.

▶ Solve each problem.

1. 2)24̄ (12)

2. 6 × 7 = 42

3. 3)36̄ (12)

4. 38 + 17 = 55

5. 83 − 47 = 36

6. 57 + 34 = 91

7. 8 × 4

8. 4 × 7

9. 7)70̄

10. 804 − 238

11. 132 − 78

12. 176 + 394

Plant a family vegetable garden. Make a list of questions about planting a garden. Show your list of questions to an adult family member. Where can you find the answers?

▶ **Write the correct compound word from the word bank on each line to complete the story.**

| nighttime | outside | backyard | doghouse | butterfly | weekends |

I like the _____ because I get to

spend time _____ with my dog

Rusty. In the morning, Rusty comes out of his _____

to play. We play in the _____ . Rusty likes to

bark at the _____ that lives in the garden.

When _____ comes, Rusty and I are

ready to sleep!

Have you ever heard of a spoon and bottle band? Find some spoons and bottles. With a family member, discover how to make music with spoons and bottles. Then, share your spoon and bottle band music with your family.

▶ **Symmetry** occurs when two halves of a figure match exactly when folded together. The **line of symmetry** is the location of the fold.

> **EXAMPLE:** This square shows a **line of symmetry** from top to bottom (vertical).

▶ In each group, circle the figure that has a line of symmetry.

1.

2.

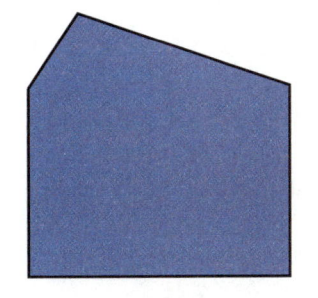 

Make a rainy day journal. Take several sheets of paper. Label each page with something fun to do on a rainy day. Then, make a drawing showing the activity. Share your rainy day journal with friends and family.

▶ **Write each word from the word bank under the correct heading.**

| buttermilk | snowstorm | replanted | peaceful | daylight |
| airplane | selection | sleepless | football | unpacked |

Compound Words   **Words with Prefixes or Suffixes**

_____   _____

_____   _____

_____   _____

_____   _____

_____   _____

Play pizza maker! Decide what kind of pizza to make. Then, take a paper plate and markers and create a drawing of a pizza. Share your special pizza with your family.

▶ **Read the passage. Then, answer the questions.**

Flash Floods

Rain is good for people and plants. When it rains too much, though, people could be in danger. A flash flood occurs when a lot of rain falls quickly, filling the streets faster than the water can drain. Driving is very dangerous in a flash flood. A person's car could be swept away. If you live in an area where flash flooding is likely, you should listen to radio or TV news reports when it starts to rain. Be ready to leave your home with your family if a newscaster says to move to higher ground. If you leave on foot, do not walk through moving water. Your parents should not drive through standing water unless it is less than six inches (15.24 cm) deep. After a flood, listen to news reports. A newscaster will tell you when you can return home safely and when the water from your tap will be safe to drink.

1. What is the main idea of this passage?

    A. Flash floods can be dangerous and occur suddenly.

    B. Never drive through a flooded area.

    C. Take important items with you when you leave your home.

2. What happens during a flash flood? _____

    _____

3. What should you do when it starts to rain? _____

    _____

4. What should you do after a flood? _____

    _____

Get each day off to a good start. Write a cheer. Share the cheer with your family. Does it make them smile?

▶ **Draw lines to divide each shape according to the fraction given.**

1. thirds

2. fourths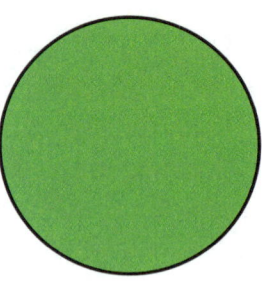

3. fifths

4. eighths

5. halves

6. tenths

Create the sounds of a summer rain and thunderstorm. Use your fingers and hands. See if you can make the sound of falling rain or a crack of thunder.

▶ **Circle each correctly spelled word. Then, write it in the blank to complete each sentence.**

1. Astronauts are _____ while they are in space.

   waitless   weightless   waghtless   wateless

2. The _____ children helped their mother rake leaves.

   thotful   toughtful   thoughtful   thowghtful

3. You need to remember to keep your doctor's _____.

   apointment   apowntment   appointment

Go to the beach with your family. Be sure that everyone knows how to be safe while at the beach. Make a three-panel comic strip promoting beach safety. Share the comic strip with your family.

▶ **How much height does a ball lose with each bounce?**

Energy is the ability to do work. Potential energy is the energy that an object has because of its position. The energy of an object in motion is called kinetic energy. If you hold a tennis ball above the ground, it has potential energy due to its position. When the ball is released, gravity pulls it down. The ball's potential energy becomes kinetic energy.

Materials:
- meterstick
- tennis ball

Procedure:

Hold the meterstick vertically with one end against the floor. Hold the tennis ball so that the bottom is at the zero mark.

Drop the ball from a height of 1 meter. Watch carefully to determine the height of the first, second, and third bounces. Round the answer to the nearest centimeter and record the information in the table below.

Bounce	Height of Bounce
1	
2	
3	

What Is This All About?

The shape of the tennis ball changes slightly when it hits the floor. Some energy is lost as heat (due to friction from air resistance) and when the ball changes shape. Because of the lost energy, the ball will not bounce to the same height it was dropped from.

What is your all-time favorite book to read? Make a list of five reasons why you like this book so much. Then, share your list with a family member and talk about your reasons.

▶ Write >, <, or = in the circle to make a true math statement.

1. $\frac{2}{3}\ \bigcirc\ \frac{1}{3}$

2. $\frac{12}{13}\ \bigcirc\ \frac{11}{13}$

3. $\frac{1}{12}\ \bigcirc\ \frac{1}{3}$

4. $\frac{5}{9}\ \bigcirc\ \frac{6}{9}$

5. $\frac{2}{6}\ \bigcirc\ \frac{3}{6}$

6. $\frac{2}{5}\ \bigcirc\ \frac{4}{10}$

7. $\frac{1}{4}\ \bigcirc\ \frac{2}{8}$

8. $\frac{3}{4}\ \bigcirc\ \frac{1}{4}$

9. $\frac{3}{8}\ \bigcirc\ \frac{5}{8}$

Design a mural for your neighborhood. Show your neighbors celebrating the Fourth of July together. Make a drawing of the mural. Then, share it with your family.

▶ **Beth wants to be a paramedic, and she practices on her dog, Gumbo. Read the story to see how Gumbo feels about all of this. Then, read each of the four questions. Write the letter for the best answer on the line.**

Good Old Gumbo . . .

No dog was ever as patient as Gumbo. Just ask Beth. She is his owner. Beth has put Gumbo through a great deal in his young life. He has been a model for **assorted** doll clothes. He has **retrieved** baseballs from under thick hedges. Now Gumbo is a model again. This time it is for splints and bandages.

Beth is learning all about first aid. She hopes to be a paramedic one day. She thinks helping people would be a good thing. She wants to practice every bandage and splint on Gumbo.

After only five minutes, Gumbo has become **disturbed**. He does not think being wrapped up is much fun. He decides that he had better do something **immediately**. He has heard the saying, "being all tied up." Gumbo wants to get out of this while he still can!

_____ 1. The word **assorted** means:

    A. tired   B. mixed   C. hungry   D. distant

_____ 2. The word **retrieved** means:

    A. bought   B. made   C. begged   D. brought back

_____ 3. The word **disturbed** means:

    A. upset   B. soft   C. silly   D. loud

_____ 4. The word **immediately** means:

    A. now   B. inside   C. under   D. never

Write a 30-second commercial that promotes bicycle safety. First, make a list of key bicycle safety rules. Then, write the commercial. Share it with adult family members and friends.

▶ **Read the passage and study the map. Then, answer the questions.**

Lines of latitude are imaginary lines that run east to west on a map. They are marked in degrees (°) and help people locate places around the world. The equator is the line at 0° latitude. The lines of latitude on the map below are measured in 15° segments from the equator. Places north of the equator have the letter **N** after their degrees. Places south of the equator have the letter **S** after their degrees.

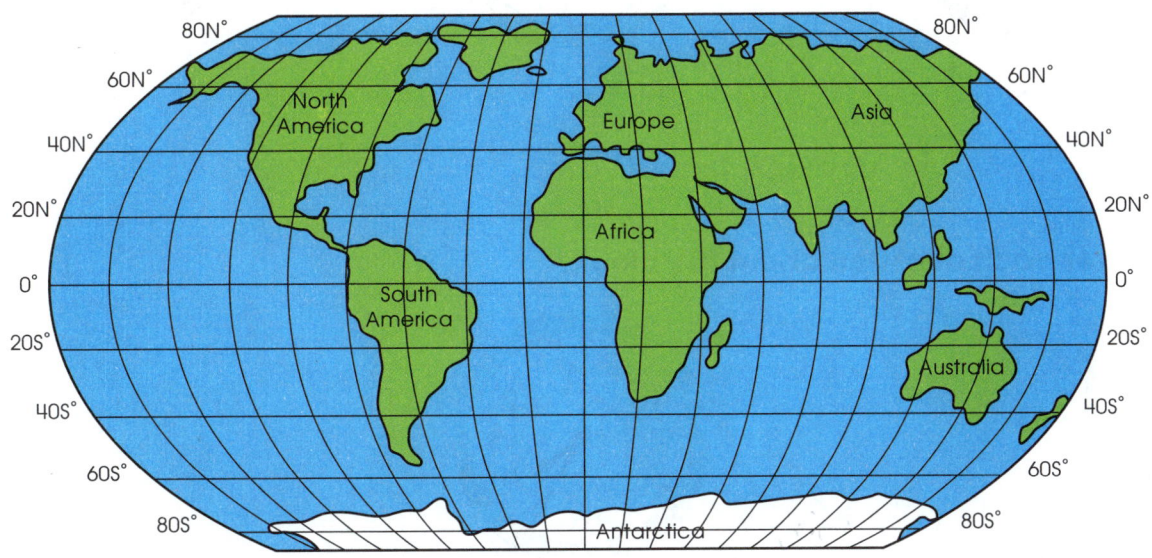

1. The equator is at _____° latitude.

2. For locations in North America, the latitude should be followed by the letter _____ .

3. The latitude for the southern tip of South America would be followed by the letter _____ .

4. Use a red crayon or marker to trace the equator.

With a family member, take a walk around your neighborhood. Note the different kinds of trees you see. Identify each tree. Make a list of trees that grow in your neighborhood. Share the list with family members.

▶ Write the time for each clock.

1.

   _____ : _____

2.

   _____ : _____

3.

   _____ : _____

▶ Answer each question about the clock.

4. What time does the clock show? _____

5. What time was it 15 minutes earlier? _____

6. What time will it be in half an hour? _____

7. What time would the clock show if you switched the hands? _____

Make a four-panel comic strip showing the different ways you could help a neighbor. Share your comic strip with family and friends.

American Education Publishing™

▶ **Read the story. Then, answer the questions.**

A Fishing Friend

It all began last summer when Davey was fishing at his grandpa's farm. Suddenly, something odd **occurred**. A big head **emerged** from the water. Davey was **terrified** at first. The creature smiled and told Davey that his name was Clarence. Clarence was a fish!

Clarence told Davey that he had always been alone and was tired of his **solitude**. He wanted a friend. Davey felt sorry for Clarence and tried his best to cheer him up.

Now it seems that Davey has a friend for life. There is just one problem: Clarence wants to be with Davey all the time. Davey cannot go fishing alone anymore. He hopes Clarence will find another new friend soon. Davey would like some of his own solitude. He would also like to catch some fish. Few fish come around when Clarence is near!

_____ 1. The word **occurred** means:

    A. pointed   B. painted   C. scraped   D. happened

_____ 2. The word **emerged** means:

    A. fell in   B. came out   C. divided   D. twisted around

_____ 3. The word **terrified** means:

    A. scared   B. rich   C. healthy   D. ripped

_____ 4. The word **solitude** means:

    A. teacher   B. friends   C. leaving   D. being alone

Plan a trip to the swimming pool. Make a list of what you will need to take with you. Be sure to include money. How much will you need? Share your list with family members. Can they add anything to your list?

▶ Use the map to find the cities located at each latitude and longitude listed below. Then, write the name of each city.

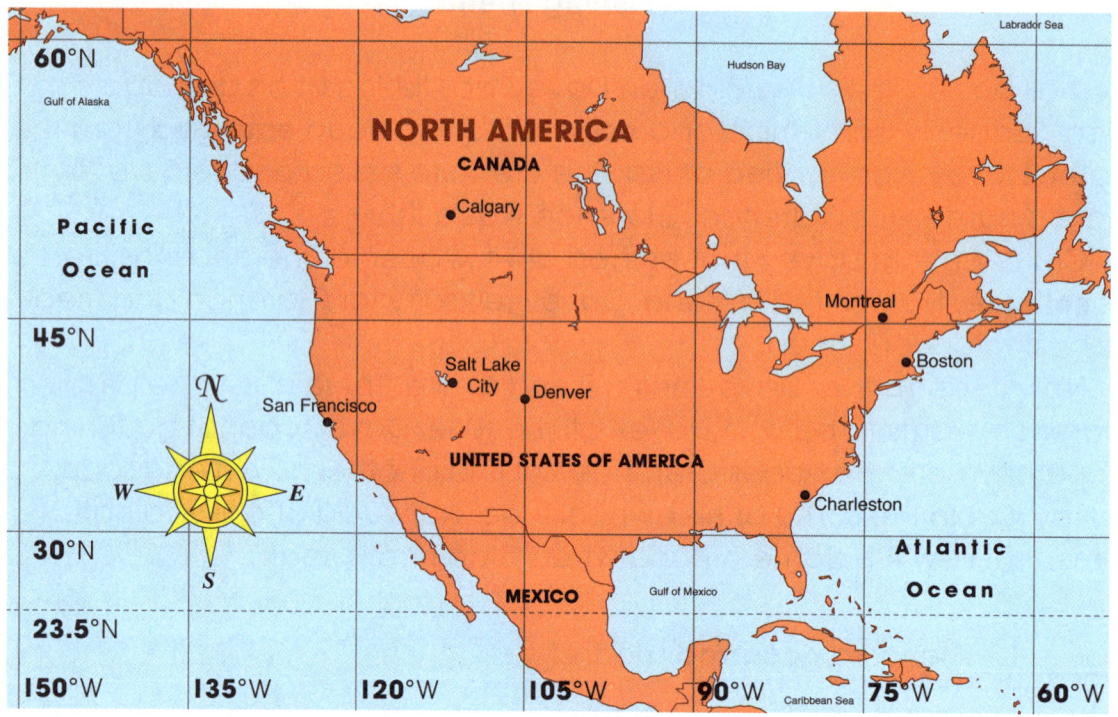

	Latitude	Longitude	City
1.	51°N	114°W	_____
2.	39°N	105°W	_____
3.	42°N	71°W	_____
4.	32°N	79°W	_____
5.	45°N	73°W	_____
6.	40°N	111°W	_____
7.	37°N	122°W	_____

If your family had a mascot, what might it be? Make a list of five possible mascots for your family. Draw a picture of each one. Show the pictures to your family members. Take a vote to determine your family's mascot.

▶ **Read each problem and circle the correct answer for each.**

1. Which clock shows 8:30?

2. Which clock has the same time as the first one?

3. Which clock shows 15 minutes before 7?

4. **Quarter past four** is another way of saying which of the following times?

Help teach your neighbor's three-year-old child how to brush his teeth. Write a fun song on the best way to brush for healthy teeth and gums. Share your song with family members.

203

American Education Publishing™

▶ **Read the paragraph. Then, draw your own coat of arms in the box.**

A Coat of Arms

A coat of arms is a design that belongs to a particular person or family. The colors, symbols, and backgrounds used in a coat of arms all have special meanings and say something about the coat of arms's owner. For example, the color blue may represent truth and loyalty, while a lion may represent courage. Create a coat of arms for yourself. Think of some qualities that you have and are proud of. Brainstorm ways that you could represent those qualities on your coat of arms. Go online with an adult if you need more information.

Write a note to a grandparent, aunt, or uncle. Tell three things you appreciate about him or her. Share your note with adult family members and then send it to the lucky person.

▶ **Study the pictograph. Then, answer the questions.**

Month	Tires Sold
Jan.	⭕⭕⭕⭕⭕☾
Feb.	⭕⭕
March	⭕☾
April	⭕⭕⭕☾
May	⭕

Key
⭕ = 500 tires

1. How many more tires were sold in April than in February?

   _____

2. What is the difference between the least number of tires sold in a month and the greatest number of tires sold in a month?

   _____

Find a comfortable place to sit with a family member. Play a game called "What's that sound?" Take a blindfold and cover the eyes of one person. The other person makes a sound with something found in the room. The blindfolded person guesses what it is. Take turns making sounds and wearing the blindfold.

▶ **Follow the directions below to learn about shadows.**

Take a tape measure outside four times throughout one day. Each time, have an adult measure the length of your shadow and record the measurements. Then, with an adult, use the computer to search for information about Earth's rotation around the sun. This will help explain why the length of your shadow changes throughout the day.

How do you find how tall a tree is without a long measuring tape and a tall ladder? You can use the measurements of a tree's shadow and the shadow of a 12-inch ruler to find the height of a tree. First, go outside with an adult and measure the length of a tree's shadow with a measuring tape, yardstick, or meterstick. Then, stand the ruler on its end at a 90° angle from the ground. Use the measuring tape, a yardstick, or a meterstick to find the length of the ruler's shadow. Record the length of each shadow and convert the measurements to the same unit, such as inches. To find the height of the tree, divide the length of the tree's shadow by the length of the ruler's shadow. Then, multiply the answer by the length of the ruler.

For example, if the answer is 10, this means that the tree's shadow is 10 times longer than the ruler, which makes the tree about 10 feet tall.

Create a new dance. It is a dance for people to do all through the day. What kind of dance would you suggest doing? Decide on a dance and then practice doing it. Share it with your family.

▶ Read each problem and circle the correct answer. Use extra paper to help you solve the problems if needed.

1. Jarvis has 5 quarters, 10 dimes, 3 nickels, and 37 pennies. How much money does he have?

    $2.50 $2.67 $2.77 $3.77

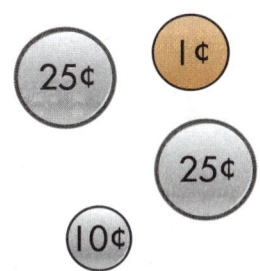

2. Michael has $6.25. If he rents a video game for $4.75, how much change will he have?

    $2.50 $2.75 $1.25 $1.50

3. Michelle wants to purchase an $11.00 baseball cap, a $15.00 shirt, and a $1.00 pack of gum. She has a $50.00 bill. How much change will she receive?

    $27.00 $23.00 $77.00 $50.00

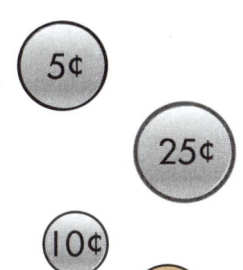

Write a new phone message greeting for your family. The greeting should use exactly ten words. Share your ten-word phone message greeting with your family.

▶ **Read the story. Then, answer the questions.**

Ike, Spike, and the Circle Game

Ike and Spike are two brave little boys who will try anything once. There is just one problem. These nine-year-old friends can never agree. They always want to do things in different ways. That is quite a **dilemma** sometimes!

Once, they **created** a large mural. Ike's faces were smiling, and Spike's faces all frowned. Another day, the boys went for a long hike. Ike took the path up into the hills, and Spike walked down by the river. They did not find each other again until the next day.

Today they are **struggling** to get home from a fishing **excursion**. Each boy wants to go a different way. These poor guys have been spinning in circles for an hour. Maybe soon one will get tired so they can at least move the boat!

_____ 1. The word **dilemma** means:

    A. canoe   B. problem   C. bait   D. song

_____ 2. The word **created** means:

    A. made   B. heard   C. told   D. found

_____ 3. The word **struggling** means:

    A. laughing   B. running   C. trying hard   D. painting

_____ 4. The word **excursion** means:

    A. hat   B. lesson   C. trip   D. fort

_____ 5. A word in the story that is a synonym for **varied** is:

    A. ordinary   B. poor   C. problem   D. different

What is your favorite kind of juice? Make a list of the reasons you like the juice. Then, write a 30-second commercial that promotes your favorite kind of juice. Share it with adult family members. Are they ready to drink a glass of juice with you?

▶ **Read the paragraph. Then, answer the questions.**

Back to School!

Sandra's mother offered to help her get ready for the new school year. Sandra grew a full inch taller over the summer. Her shoes were too tight, and her pants were almost above her ankles.

1. What do you think Sandra and her mother will do? _____

   _____

   _____

   _____

2. Which clues helped you decide? _____

   _____

   _____

   _____

Night after night, you spend time in your bed. Write a thank-you note to your bed. Let your bed know how much you appreciate its support. Read your note to a family member.

▶ **Complete the table.**

	Total Price	Amount Given to Clerk	Change Received
EXAMPLE:	$1.35	$1.50	$0.15
1.	$2.50	$5.00	
2.	$0.95	$1.00	
3.	$1.80	$2.00	
4.	$6.42	$10.00	
5.	$9.35	$20.00	
6.	$5.55	$6.00	
7.	$13.95	$20.00	
8.	$85.00	$100.00	

Plan a picnic! Make a list of what you will pack for the picnic. Decide where it will be and who to invite. Share your picnic plan with an adult family member.

▶ **Write the base word of each word.**

1. playful _____

2. disinterest _____

3. rewrite _____

4. uncover _____

5. spoonful _____

6. quickly _____

7. happiness _____

8. doubtful _____

9. kindness _____

10. recover _____

Plan a party for a friend. Make a four-panel comic strip showing how you would prepare for the party. Post your comic strip for family members to view. Are they ready to hire you to plan a party?

211

Underline the adjectives in each paragraph below. The first adjective has been underlined for you.

1. I like <u>chocolate</u> ice cream. Chocolate ice cream tastes good when it is hot outside. Unfortunately, chocolate ice cream makes a big, sticky mess. I solve this problem by eating my yummy, chocolate ice cream outside.

2. One sunny day, I found a white rabbit hopping in front of my house. I walked up to the frightened rabbit and talked to him. He finally calmed down and I picked him up. His soft fur tickled my hands. I took the sweet rabbit behind my house to the big forest. Waiting there for him was his happy mother. The two small rabbits hopped home together.

Which do you prefer to use when drawing a picture: pencil, pen, crayon, or marker? Take a poll of your family members and friends to see which they prefer.

▶ **Read the passage. Then, answer the questions.**

Food Webs

A food web is a drawing that shows how different living things are connected. In a food web, the living things at the bottom are eaten by the animals directly above them. For example, a food web might start at the bottom with plants. Plants do not eat other living things. Above these plants might be small animals, such as mice, that eat plants. Larger animals, such as owls and snakes, eat mice. A food web can tell us what might happen if certain plants or animals disappear from an ecosystem, or the surroundings in which all of the plants and animals live. In the food web described above, if something happened to the plants, then the mice would not have as much food. This would affect the owls and snakes, who would also not have enough food. Soon, there would be fewer of each type of animal. This is why it is important to protect all living things in an ecosystem, not just the larger ones.

1. What is the main idea of this passage?

    A. Food webs show how all living things are connected.

    B. Owls and snakes are the most important animals.

    C. Only the animals at the top of the food web should be protected.

2. What is a food web? _____

   _____

3. What might happen if the plants in a food web disappear? _____

   _____

Make a list of places you have been where you heard background music playing. Share your list with family members. Can they add places to the list?

▶ **Use the information in the box to help you find each equivalent measurement.**

2 cups = 1 pint	4 quarts = 1 gallon
2 pints = 1 quart	16 cups = 1 gallon

1. 5 quarts = _____ pints

2. 3 gallons = _____ pints

3. 4 cups = _____ pints

4. 2 pints = _____ cups

5. _____ gallons = 16 pints

6. 5 gallons = _____ quarts

7. _____ pints = 2 quarts

8. 3 quarts = _____ cups

You are the sandwich chef for the day. Draw a picture of your special sandwich. Top the sandwich with a smiley face. What ingredients might you use to make the sandwich's smiley face? Post your picture for family members to enjoy.

Read the story. Then, answer the questions.

Friends to the End

Tussie and Gordy are the best of friends. After all, they are the two largest and loudest creatures in the jungle. There was a time when they feared each other. Now, they find that they can **actually** help each other. Sometimes Gordy will scrub Tussie's huge, gray back. Tussie returns the **favor** by making her trunk into a shower for Gordy.

Once, they **combined** efforts to do something quite **noble**. A newborn tiger cub had wandered into the jungle. The cub's parents were worried and came to Gordy and Tussie for help. Tussie made big, wide paths through the thick jungle. Gordy swung from tree to tree looking everywhere. Together, in an hour's time, they found the tiger cub. Everyone was pleased!

_____ 1. The word **actually** means:

   A. slowly   B. hotly   C. angrily   D. really

_____ 2. The word **favor** means:

   A. drink   B. good deed   C. surprise   D. dark night

_____ 3. The word **combined** means:

   A. pointed   B. slid   C. joined   D. yelled

_____ 4. The word **noble** means:

   A. furry   B. good   C. calm   D. bad

Imagine the clocks in your home could talk. Pick two clocks in your home that are in the same room. Create a four-panel comic strip showing the clocks having a funny conversation. Post your comic strip for family members to enjoy.

▶ **Follow the directions below to create your own obstacle course.**

Boost your endurance and help a friend or family member get fit too. Make an outdoor obstacle course using soft objects, such as piles of leaves, to run around and hop over. Mark a turnaround spot so that you can retrace your hops and repeat the course. Use two strong, soft pieces of fabric to tie yourself to your partner above the ankles and knees. Remember that you must work together to complete this course. For the first time through, walk the route and discuss your strategy. For the following turn, time your performance. Then, set a goal and repeat the course to try to beat your time. Encourage each other to challenge yourselves. Keep going until you reach your goal!

Keep your family healthy. One way to do this is by frequently washing your hands for 20 seconds. Make a two-column chart, labeling one column "Family Member" and the other column "Time." Place the chart along with a timer near the kitchen sink. Have family members time themselves each time they wash their hands.

▶ **Complete each fact family.**

1. 5 × 3 = _____

   _____ × _____ = _____

   _____ ÷ _____ = _____

   _____ ÷ _____ = _____

2. 21 ÷ 3 = _____

   _____ ÷ _____ = _____

   _____ × _____ = _____

   _____ × _____ = _____

3. 30 ÷ 6 = _____

   _____ ÷ _____ = _____

   _____ × _____ = _____

   _____ × _____ = _____

Have you ever watched someone clean a sink? Create a five-panel comic strip showing the step-by-step directions for cleaning a sink. Then, post your comic strip for your family to view.

▶ **Circle the adverb in each sentence. Underline the verb each adverb modifies.**

1. The dogs barked loudly at the sound of the doorbell.

2. I looked everywhere for my coat.

3. Nancy swims faster than I do.

4. Greg walked slowly up the driveway.

5. Valerie awoke early on Saturday morning.

6. Let's play outside in the front yard.

Form a band! What instruments would you have in the band? What kind of music would you play? What would be the name of the band? Write a note to a family member telling about your band.

▶ **Find each probability.**

> Chloe has 11 pencils in her pencil box. Two pencils are orange, 3 pencils are blue, 5 pencils are yellow, and 1 pencil is green.

1. What is the probability that Chloe will pull out a black pencil?

   _____

2. What is the probability that Chloe will pull out an orange pencil?

   _____

3. What is the probability that Chloe will pull out a green pencil?

   _____

4. What is the probability that Chloe will pull out a blue pencil?

   _____

5. What is the probability that Chloe will pull out a yellow pencil?

   _____

6. What color pencil is Chloe most likely to pull out of her pencil box?

   _____

Make a list of five healthy things you can do today. Then, create a five-panel comic strip showing your healthy actions. Post your comic strip for family members to see.

American Education Publishing™

Read the passage. Then, answer the questions.

Edward Murrow

Edward Murrow was an American journalist. He became famous during World War II. Murrow was born in 1908 in North Carolina. After college, he began working for a radio station. Many Americans listened to his live broadcasts during the bombing of London, England, in September 1939. Before Murrow's reports, people in the United States learned about the war through newsreels in movie theaters or articles in newspapers. Now, they could learn about the war in London as it was happening. After the war, Murrow worked as a reporter in radio, then in television. He became known for interviewing, or asking questions of, important people. Other newscasters followed in Murrow's footsteps. Today, we still rely on reporters in other countries for news and information. And, we still listen to reporters' conversations with famous people.

1. What is the main idea of this passage?

    A. Edward Murrow was a brave American journalist.

    B. Edward Murrow talked to many famous people.

    C. Edward Murrow worked in London.

2. How did people learn about the war before Murrow's reports?

    _____

3. How did Murrow change the way journalists work?

    _____

    _____

Plan a Fourth of July barbecue. Design an invitation for the event. Be sure to include time and place along with the RSVP to help you know how many will attend. Show your invitation to your family. Do they like the idea of a barbecue?

▶ **Study the bar graph. Then, answer each question.**

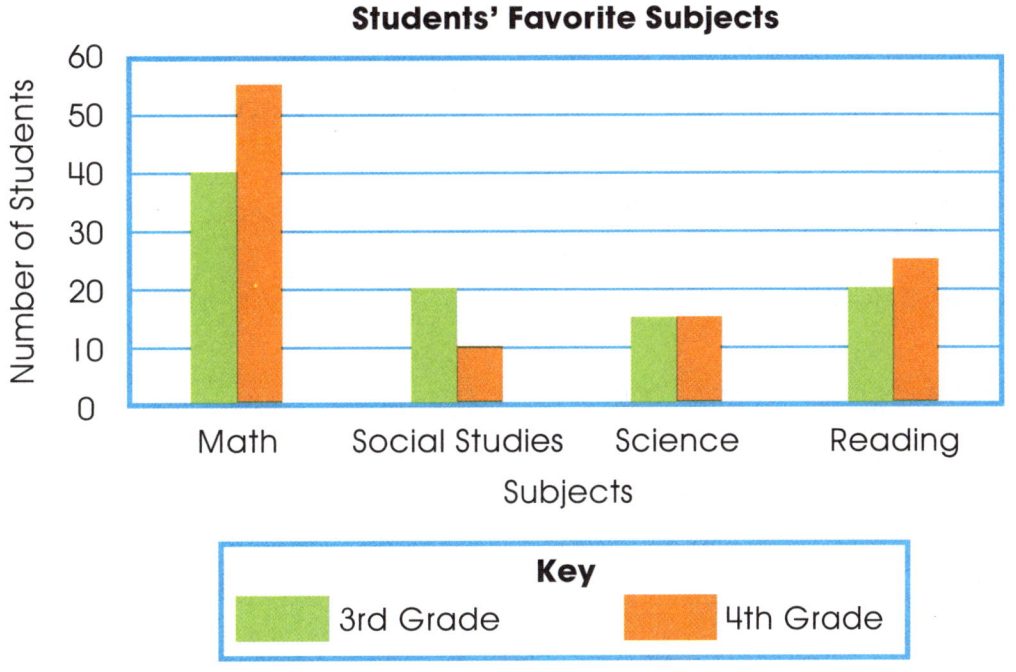

1. What is the total number of students who like social studies?

   _____

2. How many total students are in 3rd grade? Fourth grade?

   _____

3. Which subject has the greatest difference between 3rd and 4th grade?

   _____

4. How many more students like math than reading in 3rd grade? Fourth grade?

   _____

Your best friend is having a party. You will not be able to attend. Write a note to your friend telling why you will not be at the party. Share your note with your friends.

▶ **Adverbs** tell when, where, how, or to what extent. Use your imagination to complete the story with adverbs.

News travels _____ in my school. On the day I won 100 ice-cream cone coupons, _____ everybody was my friend. Marty came _____ up to me. She begged me for a chocolate cone. I told her _____ that I would think about it. Fernando came _____. He got _____ on his knees and begged _____. Jill offered to trade me her bubble gum for a strawberry ice cream coupon, but I said, "No, thanks." Wow, people sure act _____ sometimes.

I _____ do want to share my ice cream, I just want to wait _____.

Go on a job hunt! Ask an adult family member to help you make a list of adult family members, including grandparents and aunts and uncles. Next to each name, write the kind of work each family member does or did. What did you learn about your family by doing this job search?

▶ **The bar graph below shows how many boxes of cookies were sold at Discovery Elementary School over an eight-week period. Use the graph to answer the questions.**

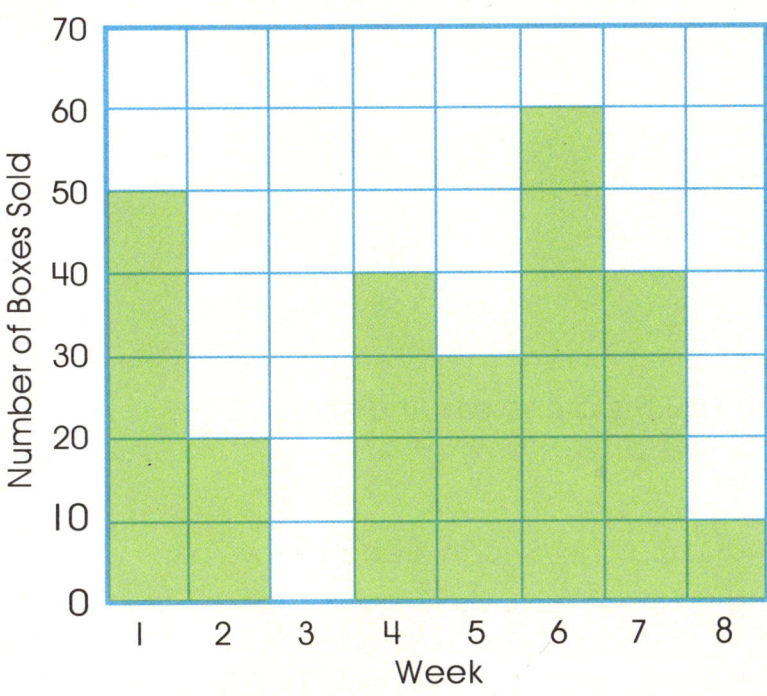

1. What was the total number of boxes sold during the eight-week sale? _____

2. During which two weeks were the same number of boxes sold? _____

3. How many more boxes were sold during week 6 than week 7? _____

4. How many fewer boxes were sold during week 8 than week 2? _____

5. How many boxes were sold during week 3? _____ What do you think might have happened? _____

You are grown up and have a job. Write a note to a family member telling about your work. Where do you work? What are you doing? What do you enjoy about the work? Share your note with family members.

Add commas where they belong in each phrase or sentence.

1. My family visits Spring Grove, Minnesota every year in the summer.

2. Dear Grandpa,

3. Yours truly,

4. On October 9, 2009, Carolyn saw the play.

5. My aunt and uncle live in North Branch, New York.

6. Dear Jon,

7. January 1, 2010

8. Paris, Texas is located in the northeastern part of the state.

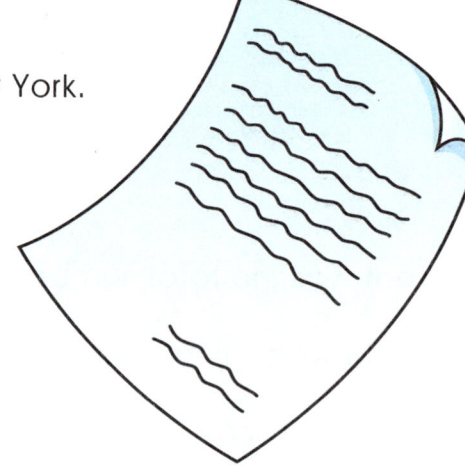

Write a recipe for a fun summer day. What do you think makes for a fun day? Make a three-panel comic strip showing a fun summer day. Post your comic strip for family members to view.

▶ **Divide to find each quotient.**

1. 3)18   2. 4)24   3. 3)21

4. 4)36   5. 8)32   6. 5)40

7. 6)36   8. 9)36   9. 8)40

Write a sports update providing the scores from yesterday's key sporting events and any other interesting sports news. Deliver the sports news to your family members.

▶ **Read the story. Then, answer the questions.**

A Special Birthday Gift

Ivy's grandmother will celebrate her 70th birthday soon. Ivy wants to get her grandmother a special gift, but she spent her money on new books instead. Ivy loves reading about Mexico. Her grandmother came from Mexico, and she read to Ivy when Ivy was little. Lately, her grandmother's eyesight has been failing, so she can no longer see the words on the page.

1. What do you think Ivy will do? _____

   _____

   _____

   _____

2. Which clues helped you decide? _____

   _____

   _____

   _____

Design a new game called "Home Inspector." Start by making a list of the rooms in your home. Then, decide what the rules of the game will be. Share your "Home Inspector" game plan with family and friends. What fun ideas do they have to add to the game?

Complete each sentence with the correct word from the parentheses.

1. The baseball game went _____ for the Spartans right from the first inning. (well, better, best)

2. The first batter, Monroe, always hits _____ . (well, better, best)

3. Monroe runs the bases _____ than most players on his team. (well, better, best)

4. Stanley, the second batter, usually hits even _____ than Monroe. (well, better, best)

5. The pitcher threw his _____ pitches to Stanley. (well, better, best)

6. Stanley hit the ball _____, and it flew over the fence for a two-run home run. (well, better, best)

7. Things went _____ for the Tigers in the second half of the game than in the first. (badly, worse, worst)

Make a sign to put on your door. The purpose of the sign is to let family members know what you are doing and where you are. When you finish the sign, post it and let your family members know.

▶ **Solve each word problem. Show your work.**

1. Bobbi made 8 quarts of punch for the party. How many cups did she make?

2. Two boxes of gold weigh 4 pounds 8 ounces. Each pound costs $400. How much are the boxes worth in all?

3. Ms. Lackey gave each student in her class a calculator. Each calculator weighed 16 ounces. If Ms. Lackey gave each of her 20 students a calculator, how many pounds did the calculators weigh in all?

4. Virginia's school ordered 20 boxes of milk. In each box, there were 35 containers of milk. By the end of the week, 265 containers were used. How many containers were left?

Have you ever thought about your pillow and what a good friend it is? Make a three-panel comic strip telling about your good friend Pillow. Post your comic strip for friends and family to enjoy.

▶ **Follow the directions below to learn a new version of freeze tag.**

Get fit with this version of freeze tag! Invite several friends or family members to play. Start by choosing someone to be "it." That person must chase and tag everyone until all of the players are "frozen." Frozen players perform an ongoing exercise, such as jumping jacks or running in place. Players who are free can unfreeze their teammates by tapping them on their shoulders. The last person frozen becomes "it." Continue playing until everyone has gotten a good endurance-boosting workout.

Your best friend's family has just joined a new health club. It has a big swimming pool, and it even has an indoor climbing wall. Write a note to your adult family members telling them why you think it would be a good idea for your family to join the health club.

▶ **Read each sentence. List each word on the line beside the correct part of speech.**

1. These berries smash easily.

   noun _____   adjective _____

   verb _____   adverb _____

2. Ten soldiers march together.

   noun _____   adjective _____

   verb _____   adverb _____

3. The big pillow belongs here.

   noun _____   adjective _____

   verb _____   adverb _____

Build a word pyramid. Start by writing down a word that has one letter. On the next line, write a two-letter word. Continue building your pyramid by increasing the number of letters in a each word. How big can you make your pyramid?

Read the story. Then, write the meaning of each word.

Different Homes

Gabe lives in a large city with his grandparents. The building that he and his grandparents live in is very tall and has different sets of rooms for each family that lives there. This building is called an apartment building. In this **community**, all of the buildings are close together. People do not have to go far to get things they need in this **urban** area. Gabe's cousin, Jasper, lives in a **rural**, or country, community. He plays in his large backyard instead of in a park like Gabe. There is a lot of space between houses where Jasper lives. Both Gabe's and Jasper's neighborhoods have schools, hospitals, and stores.

1. community _____

   _____

   _____

2. urban _____

   _____

   _____

3. rural _____

   _____

   _____

Create a new super hero. What would its name be? What would it look like? What would it be able to do? How would it help people? Draw a picture of your super hero. Share it with family and friends.

▶ **Use the word bank to label each part of the friendly letter.**

| body | closing | greeting | signature | heading |

__heading__ { 1921 King Street
Boise, Idaho 83704
August 2, 2009

__greeting__ Dear Sara,

__body__ { I am having a great time at camp.
I swim every day and hike a lot too.
Yesterday, our group hiked five miles.
I hope you are feeling better.

__closing__ Your friend,

__signature__ Fiona

Go on a scavenger hunt for books! Take paper and a pencil. Walk around your home looking for books. Make a tally mark for each book you find. How many did you find? Share the results of your book hunt with your family.

▶ **Read the passage. Then, answer the questions.**

Early Computers

Have you ever used a computer at school, at the library, or at home? Today, a computer can fit on a desktop or in your lap. A computer of the past took up a whole room! One of the first computers was called the ENIAC, which stood for Electronic Numerical Integrator and Calculator. It took up 1,800 square feet (about 167 sq. m), weighed nearly 50 tons, and cost $500,000. The ENIAC took three years to build and was designed for the U.S. Army. It required a team of six people to program it, or tell it what to do. The ENIAC was used from 1947 to 1955. In contrast, a personal computer today can weigh less than 2 pounds (about 1 kg) and can be operated by one person at a time.

1. What is the main idea of this passage?

    A. The ENIAC was an early computer.

    B. Computers of the past were very different from computers today.

    C. Students can do their homework on computers.

2. How large was ENIAC? _____

3. When was the ENIAC used? _____

4. How are computers today different from those in the past? _____

_____

_____

_____

Design a treasure hunt for your family members. Take paper and a pencil. Write the step-by-step directions guiding them to some place in your home where a treasure awaits discovery. What might that treasure be? Have fun creating the treasure hunt and sharing it with your family.

▶ **Write the number of sides and vertices for each polygon.**

1.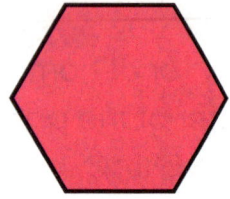

   ____sides ____vertices

2.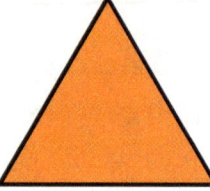

   ____sides ____vertices

3.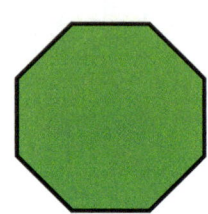

   ____sides ____vertices

4.

   ____sides ____vertices

5.

   ____sides ____vertices

6.

   ____sides ____vertices

You are a master chef. Create a delicious meal for a family member. Look through old magazines and cut out pictures of foods. Glue the pictures on a paper plate and serve them to a family member.

▶ **Write a letter to your favorite actor or actress. Include all five parts of a friendly letter. Remember to put a comma after the greeting and closing.**

You own a recycling company. Create a catchy slogan and song that encourages people to recycle. Share your slogan and song with family and friends.

In each sentence, underline the cause and circle the effect.

EXAMPLE:

The sky became cloudy, then it started to snow.

1. The cold weather caused frost to cover the windows.

2. The falling snowflakes made my cheeks wet and cold.

3. Snow stuck to my mittens because I had made a snowman.

4. The snowman melted from the heat of the sun.

5. I swam so long in the pool that I needed to put on more sunscreen.

6. Cayce missed the bus because she overslept.

7. Because Shay watched a scary movie on TV, she could not fall asleep.

8. The lady was thirsty, so she went to get a glass of water.

Build a tent! Talk with an adult family member about a good place to build a tent out of blankets. What blankets do you have that would be good for building a tent? Then, get the blankets and have fun building the tent!

▶ **Choose the best unit of measurement for each liquid.**

1. a bowl of soup
   A. cup
   B. quart
   C. pint
   D. gallon

2. a swimming pool
   A. cup
   B. quart
   C. pint
   D. gallon

3. a pitcher of water
   A. cup
   B. quart
   C. pint
   D. gallon

4. a glass of juice
   A. milliliter
   B. centiliter
   C. liter
   D. kiloliter

5. water in a bathtub
   A. milliliter
   B. centiliter
   C. liter
   D. kiloliter

6. motor oil
   A. milliliter
   B. centiliter
   C. liter
   D. kiloliter

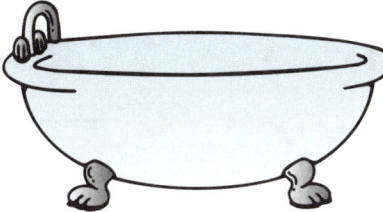

Go to a window in your home that gives you a good view of the outdoors. Imagine there was a window box filled with flowers at that window. Draw a picture of how the window would look with a window box filled with flowers. Share the picture with your family members.

▶ **Address the envelope below using the information given.**

The sender is:

Dr. James Madison

38 Carlton Place

Salem, NC 29532

The receiver is:

Ms. Mary Morton

149 Sparrow Street

Tucson, AZ 52974

Is it time for you to clean your bedroom? Make a three-panel comic strip showing your action plan for cleaning the room. Share your comic strip with family members. Invite them to join you in cleaning your room.

▶ **Circle the pronouns in each sentence.**

1. I told her about Janelle's horse.

2. This piece of cake is for him.

3. Liz invited Garrett and me to the party.

4. The table is set for us.

5. We are too late to see the first show.

6. They will be happy to come with us.

7. Clams and turtles have shells. They are protected by them.

You have a garden that has way too many weeds. Write an ad for a weed puller. Then, draw a "before" and "after" picture of your garden.

Read the passage. Then, answer the questions.

Planning a City

What do the streets in your city look like? Some cities have streets that are very straight and organized. It is easy to get from one point in the city to another. Other cities have streets that seem to go nowhere. It may be difficult to give directions to your home.

In the past, when a group of people moved to a place and started planning the streets, some of them used something called a grid system. One example of this is found in the city of Philadelphia, Pennsylvania, which is divided into four sections around a central square. The map was laid out by William Penn in 1682. The grid included wide streets that were easy for people to walk down. Penn left London, England, after a fire destroyed most of the city. London had a maze of narrow streets that were hard to move around safely. Penn wanted to make sure that people could get around easily and safely. Many other people followed Penn's ideas when setting up their new cities' street systems.

1. What is the main idea of this passage?
    A. William Penn drew the first grid system.
    B. Planning a city is important for safety and ease of use.
    C. Some streets are straight and organized.

2. What is one good thing about having straight streets? _____
_____

3. How are Philadelphia's streets different from London's? _____
_____

You and a friend are going to play catch. Where would be a good place to play? What might you use to play catch? Write a journal entry about the playing-catch adventure you might have with a friend.

▶ **Address the envelope below using the information given.**

The sender is:

Mr. Fred Barrow
216 Dawson Drive
Ogden, UT 66065

The receiver is:

Ms. Carla George
22 W. 42nd Street
Tampa, FL 21563

Take a big sheet of paper and markers. Draw a picture that covers most of the paper. Next, create a jigsaw puzzle. Determine how many pieces you want in the puzzle and then cut. Share your jigsaw puzzle with family and friends.

▶ **A figure is symmetrical if it can be folded in half so that the two parts are congruent. Draw one line of symmetry for each figure.**

1.

2.

3.

4.

Go with an adult family member to a local park. Be on the lookout for butterflies. When you spot a butterfly, run with it. After your park visit, write about your run with the butterflies. Share it with family members.

▶ **Unscramble the words in parentheses to complete each analogy.**

1. Pillows are to soft as boards are to _____ . (rdha)

2. Bells are to ring as car horns are to _____ . (nkho)

3. Hear is to ears as touch is to _____ . (serinfg)

4. Star is to pointed as circle is to _____ . (dunor)

5. Fish is to swim as bird is to _____ . (ylf)

6. Elephant is to large as mouse is to _____ . (malsl)

7. Paint is to brush as draw is to _____ . (cienlp)

Design a new sock puppet. To get started, find an old sock. Decide how you can transform the sock into a puppet and then do it. Give your sock puppet a name and share it with family and friends.

▶ **Use the table to answer each question.**

Student Music Lesson Schedule

Day 1 (new students only)	Day 2	Day 3	Day 4	Day 5
Nicole	José	Solina	Greg	Jamie
Naomi	Kira	Jamie	Kipley	Solina
Tanya	Kipley	Greg	Jacob	Rebecca
Michelle	Mark	Rebecca	José	Mark
Fiora	Jacob	Margaret	Kira	Drake

1. Other than Jacob, who has a lesson on day 4? _____

2. Tanya, Naomi, and Fiora all have a lesson on which day? _____

3. How many lessons is Jacob scheduled for in all? _____

4. Kipley, Naomi, and Mark practice together. Who is the new music student?
   _____

5. How many new students are there altogether? _____

6. Why does Mark not have a lesson on day 1? _____

Invite an adult family member to be a cloud watcher with you. Go outside and take a good look at the daytime sky. Be careful not to look directly at the sun. What do you notice about the clouds? Talk about the clouds you observe.

▶ **If you could be any animal, which animal would you be? Why?**

_____
_____
_____
_____
_____
_____
_____
_____
_____
_____
_____
_____

Be brave and take a look under your bed. What do you see? You might need to get a flashlight to see even better. Make a list of what you see. Share the list with family members and then clean under your bed!

▶ **Does the dotted line in each figure represent a line of symmetry? Circle yes or no.**

1.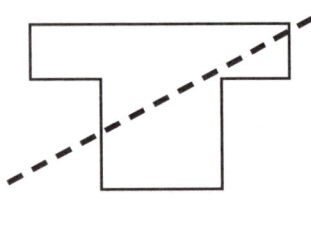

   yes   no

2.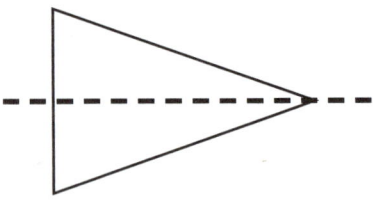

   yes   no

3.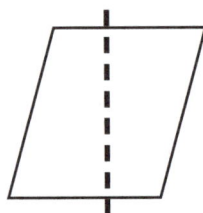

   yes   no

4.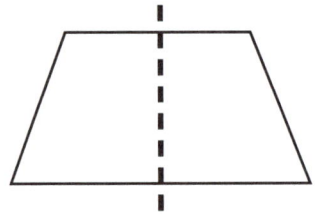

   yes   no

5.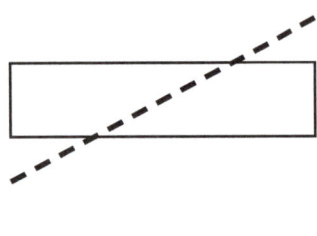

   yes   no

6.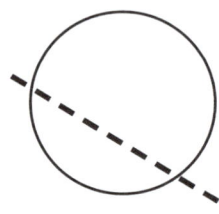

   yes   no

Think about the different ways you have helped around your home. Take three small pieces of paper. On each paper, list a different way you have been a home helper. Fold each paper and then pick one. What is next? Do what is on the paper you picked!

▶ A *table* is a compact, orderly arrangement of facts or figures, usually presented in rows or columns. Use this table to answer the questions below.

Ross's Movie Rental Review

	Sun.	Mon.	Tues.	Wed.	Thurs.	Fri.	Sat.
Chuckie Chipmunk	1	4	0	2	3	5	2
Swamp Critters	2	3	1	2	0	2	3
Hero for a Day	0	6	2	1	4	5	5
Scary Vegetables	1	2	2	4	0	3	4
Halloween Howl	1	3	2	0	0	2	2

The numbers tell how many times each movie was rented each day.

1. Which movie was not rented on Wednesday or Thursday? _____

2. Were more movies rented on Saturday or Sunday? _____

3. Was *Chuckie Chipmunk* rented more than *Halloween Howl*? _____

4. On what day were the fewest movies rented? _____

5. Which two days had seven movie rentals each? _____

Go to where the laundry is done. Observe your family member fold the laundry. Pantomime the actions you see. Then, begin folding some laundry. Talk about what you learned about folding laundry.

▶ **Complete each sentence with the correct form of *good* or *bad* from the parentheses.**

1. The weatherperson said that we will have _____ weather on Thursday. (good, better, best)

2. She said that the weather this weekend will be _____ than today. (good, better, best)

3. Sunday will have the _____ weather this week. (good, better, best)

4. Parts of the country are having _____ storms. (bad, worse, worst)

5. The weatherperson is predicting that the _____ of the snow is coming soon. (bad, worse, worst)

6. Florida usually has _____ weather in the winter. (good, better, best)

Create a funny four-panel comic strip. The topic is about sweeping the floors at home. Think about something funny that might happen with a broom or vacuum cleaner. Then, take a sheet of paper and markers and create the funny comic strip. Share your comic strip with family members.

▶ **Read the passage. Then, answer the questions.**

Magnets

A magnet is an object with a magnetic field. This means that it pulls things made of iron, steel, or nickel toward it. If you place a paper clip next to a magnet on a table, the paper clip will move toward the magnet. Every magnet has what is called a north pole and a south pole. The north pole of one magnet will stick to the south pole of another magnet. If you try to push the south poles of two magnets together, they will spring apart. Earth has magnetic poles too. Earth is a big magnet! Earth's magnetic poles are not actual places. They are areas of Earth's magnetic field that have a certain property. Although Earth's magnetic poles are different from the poles where polar bears and penguins live, its magnetic poles are near those poles. The north pole of a magnet will always try to point toward Earth's north magnetic pole. A device called a compass works by having a magnetized needle that points toward Earth's magnetic north pole. If you place a compass on a flat surface, the needle should point north.

1. What is the main idea of this passage?
    A. Every magnet has a north pole and a south pole.
    B. Compasses work by pointing to the north.
    C. A magnet is an object with a magnetic field.

2. How is Earth like a magnet? _____
   _____

3. How does a compass work? _____
   _____

Have you ever thought of becoming a book illustrator? Find a book whose illustrations you like. Then, take paper and a pencil and copy an illustration. Share the book illustration and your picture with family members.

▶ **Add to find each sum. Write each answer in its simplest form.**

1. $\dfrac{1}{3} + \dfrac{2}{3} =$
2. $\dfrac{4}{6} + \dfrac{5}{6} =$
3. $\dfrac{1}{6} + \dfrac{1}{6} =$

4. $\dfrac{3}{6} + \dfrac{1}{6} =$
5. $\dfrac{2}{4} + \dfrac{2}{4} =$
6. $\dfrac{1}{2} + \dfrac{1}{2} =$

7. $\dfrac{5}{8} + \dfrac{3}{8} =$
8. $\dfrac{5}{5} + \dfrac{2}{5} =$
9. $\dfrac{2}{10} + \dfrac{4}{10} =$

During the early morning hours, go outside with an adult family member. Listen for the birds. Note the different bird calls. After listening for a while, imitate the bird calls.

▶ A possessive pronoun is a pronoun that shows ownership. Some possessive pronouns are shown in the word bank.

| mine | your | hers | its |
| ours | his | their | my |

▶ Write five sentences in cursive. Use a possessive pronoun from the word bank in each sentence.

1. _____

2. _____

3. _____

4. _____

5. _____

Design a new game called "Dress Up." Start by finding old clothes that would make good costumes. Then, decide what the rules of the game will be. Share your "Dress Up" game with family and friends. What fun ideas do they have to add to the game?

▶ **Solve each word problem.**

1. Dexter made $5.00 washing cars on Monday, $2.75 on Tuesday, and $6.25 on Wednesday. How much money did Dexter make in the three days of car washing?

2. Kerry ate two oranges at breakfast and half an orange at lunch. At dinner, Kerry ate the other half of the orange from lunch. How many oranges did Kerry eat?

3. Missy took 114 pictures last June, 121 last July, and 109 last August. How many pictures did Missy take last summer?

4. Sandy sold 65 books at the book sale on Thursday, 231 books on Friday, and 111 more on Saturday. How many books did Sandy sell in three days?

You just won a trip around the world! Make some postcards showing five stops you will make on your travels. Share your postcards from your imaginary travels with friends and family.

▶ Look at each underlined idiom. Then, choose the correct meaning of each sentence.

1. Cody was <u>back to square one</u> when his dog chewed his science fair project.

    A. Cody stood on a square that was labeled *one*.

    B. Cody had to start his science fair project again from the beginning.

    C. Cody was unhappy that his dog chewed up his science fair project.

2. <u>Time flies</u> when we are having fun.

    A. Time seems to go quickly when we are having fun.

    B. Time has wings and flies like a bird.

    C. Time goes slowly.

3. Torika needs to <u>toe the line</u> if she wants to go to the movies.

    A. Torika needs to behave if she wants to go to the movies.

    B. Torika needs to stand behind a line if she wants to go to the movies.

    C. Torika needs to stand in line for a movie ticket.

Write a story. Get a pair of scissors and an old magazine. Look through the magazine for a picture that sparks a story idea. Cut out the picture and glue it onto construction paper. Next, write the story. Share your story with family members.

▶ **Follow the directions below to learn about perseverance.**

The word *perseverance* means to keep going even if something is difficult. Think of someone you know whom you admire or consider a hero, such as a grandparent. Ask this person if you can conduct an interview. Ask your hero questions to try to determine what made him successful. What struggles did he overcome? What made him persevere? Write the answers to those questions. After interviewing your hero, write a key quote from him below that explains his perseverance, such as, "I always tried my best because I wanted to be my best." Post the quote where you can see it every day as a reminder to never give up.

_____

_____

_____

_____

Design a clubhouse for you and your friends. Decide the best location to build the clubhouse and then create a plan. Share your clubhouse plan with your friends.

▶ **Subtract to find each difference.**

1. $7.36
   − $3.97

2. $8.90
   − $2.49

3. $7.68
   − $4.79

4. $3.85
   − $2.79

5. $7.47
   − $4.58

6. $8.37
   − $2.09

7. $4.76
   − $2.67

8. $6.89
   − $4.78

9. $6.77
   − $2.88

Create an obstacle course for a fun afternoon with your friends. Sit down with an adult family member and talk about what could be included in the fun obstacle course.

▶ **Read the passage. Then, answer the questions.**

Parasites

Some animals get their food by living in or on other things. These animals, called parasites, do not kill the animals they live on, but they may harm or irritate them. A flea will live on a dog, cat, or other animals. The animal it lives on is called the host. The flea gets its food by sucking the other animal's blood. The flea will not harm the host, but it will make the host itch and feel uncomfortable. Some worms are also parasites. A tapeworm lives inside the body of an animal. It eats the food the host has eaten. The tapeworm can make the host very sick. Plants can be parasites, too. Mistletoe and some types of ferns live on trees, taking food and water from them.

1. What is the main idea of this passage?
   A. Parasites live on or in other living things.
   B. A flea is a parasite.
   C. Parasites can make their hosts sick.

2. How does a flea get food?
   _____

3. Where does a tapeworm live?
   _____

4. What kinds of plants can be parasites?
   _____

Pick a poem and then memorize it. What poem will it be? Select a poem and memorize it. Then, recite it for your family.

▶ **What is the best thing you did this summer?**

_____
_____
_____
_____
_____
_____
_____
_____
_____
_____
_____
_____
_____

Talk with an adult family member about making a wind chime for your home. Make a list of items found around the home that could be used to make the wind chime. Then, decide on the materials you will use and make one for your home.

▶ **Look at the following figures and find the perimeter of each.**

1.

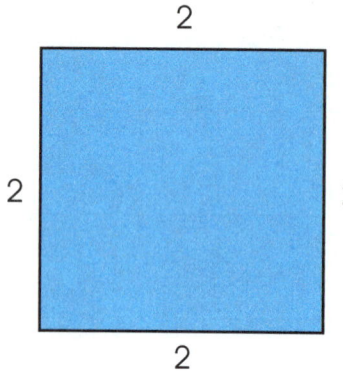

Perimeter = _____ units

2.

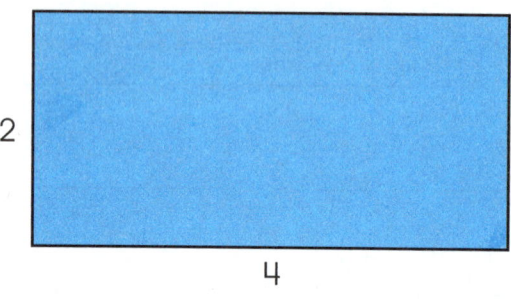

Perimeter = _____ units

Plan a clothes-swapping party. Rather than buying new clothes, people bring clothes and trade them with each other. Make a guest list of friends and neighbors to invite. Then, design the invitation. Share your invitation with your family members. Does it sound like a good idea to them?

▶ Read each sentence. Write **F** if it is a fact. Write **O** if it is an opinion.

> A **fact** is something that is real and could happen.
>
> **There are apples on the tree.**
>
> An **opinion** is something that one person may believe to be true, but another person may not agree.
>
> **Those apples are beautiful.**

_____ 1. My mother fixes dinner every night at 6:00.

_____ 2. Chocolate pie is the best dessert.

_____ 3. The state of Wisconsin is a part of the United States.

_____ 4. People can go to a movie theater to watch movies.

_____ 5. It is more fun to rent a movie and watch it at home than to go to a theater.

Do you know what a thermostat is? Ask an adult family member to show you what it is and where it is in your home. Then, check to see what the temperature is in your home. Share the temperature with your family.

▶ **Imagine that you are asked to invent a new word. What would the word be, and what would it mean?**

_____
_____
_____
_____
_____
_____
_____
_____
_____
_____
_____
_____

A good way to shop for food is to eat before you go. If you shop hungry, you might buy more food than you need. Make a three-panel comic strip showing a hungry shopper. Then, make a three-panel comic strip showing a shopper who ate before going shopping. Post your comic strips for family members to view.

▶ **Write the perimeter of each figure.**

1.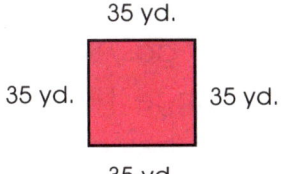

   perimeter = _____ yd.

2.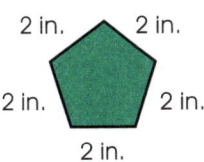

   perimeter = _____ in.

3.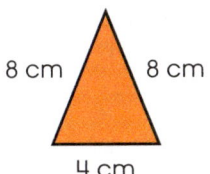

   perimeter = _____ cm

4.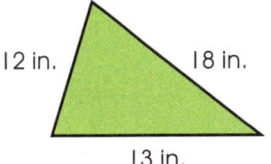

   perimeter = _____ in.

5.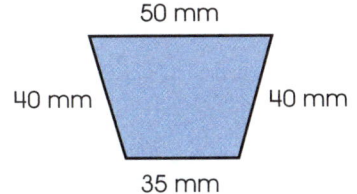

   perimeter = _____ mm

6.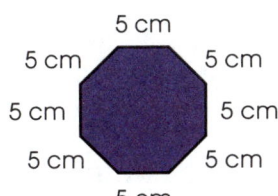

   perimeter = _____ cm

Check the weather report for the day. If it is going to be hot, plan your outfit for the day featuring lighter colors. Make a list of three light-colored clothing combinations. Show the list to your family. Which outfit do they prefer? Then, you decide on your outfit.

▶ **Read the passage. Then, answer the questions.**

Matter

All matter on Earth exists in one of three states: solid, liquid, or gas. Solids, such as boxes or books, have certain shapes that are difficult to change. Liquids, such as lemonade or orange juice, take the shape of the containers they are in. Gases, such as the air you breathe and helium, spread out to fill the space they are in. It is easy to change water from one state to another. The water you drink is a liquid. When water is heated, such as in a pot on the stove, it becomes a gas. This gas is known as steam, or vapor. Steam can be used in a large machine to make electricity. When water is frozen, such as in a tray in the freezer, it turns into ice. Ice can be used to keep drinks cold or help a hurt part of the body feel better.

1. What is the main idea of this passage?

    A. Steam is heated water.

    B. All matter exists as a solid, a liquid, or a gas.

    C. Ice cubes make water taste better.

2. What are two examples of solids? _____

3. What are two examples of liquids? _____

4. What are two examples of gases? _____

5. Water can exist as a solid, a liquid, or a gas. What is it called in each state?

   _____

With an adult family member, go for a walk in your neighborhood. Take a magnifying glass with you. Every now and then, stop and use the magnifying glass to look at familiar items. Talk about what you see.

▶ **Add to find each sum. Write each answer in simplest form.**

1. $\dfrac{1}{4} + \dfrac{3}{4} =$
2. $\dfrac{3}{5} + \dfrac{2}{5} =$
3. $\dfrac{3}{7} + \dfrac{2}{7} =$

4. $\dfrac{3}{4} + \dfrac{1}{4} =$
5. $\dfrac{1}{7} + \dfrac{1}{7} =$
6. $\dfrac{1}{6} + \dfrac{4}{6} =$

7. $\dfrac{1}{3} + \dfrac{2}{3} =$
8. $\dfrac{1}{5} + \dfrac{4}{5} =$
9. $\dfrac{2}{6} + \dfrac{2}{6} =$

Write a play to perform for an audience of pre-school children. What will you write about? How many characters will be in the play? Make a list of the characters and write a sentence about each one.

▶ **Write the correct homophone from the word bank to complete each sentence.**

| I | eye | you | ewe | wear | where |

1. My friend and _____ ate lunch together.

2. The _____ took care of her lamb.

3. Cory got a speck of dust in his _____ .

4. Do you know _____ to put the books away?

5. Would _____ please hand me that pencil?

6. Hillary will _____ her blue shoes today.

Do you have a pet? If not, imagine you have a pet. It is time to brush the pet. Write what you would say to the pet as you brush it. Then, share it with your family.

▶ Read each sentence. Write **F** if it is a fact. Write **O** if it is an opinion.

Example:

_____F_____ Abraham Lincoln was the 16th president of the United States.

1. _____ Spring is the best time of the year.

2. _____ Chocolate cake is the best dessert in the world.

3. _____ Reading is the best way to spend a rainy day.

4. _____ Dogs are the best pets.

5. _____ Neil Armstrong walked on the moon in 1969.

6. _____ Lava rock was once hot liquid.

7. _____ Eating too much candy is bad for your teeth.

8. _____ Everyone should like chocolate ice cream.

9. _____ Daytime and nighttime depend on the position of the sun in the sky.

Make a list of seven vegetables. Show your list to family members. Do they have any vegetables to add to the list? Rank the vegetables from most favorite to least favorite. What is your favorite vegetable?

▶ **Read the passage. Then, answer the questions.**

Health and Fitness

Health and fitness are important for you and your family. If you start good health habits now, you will have a better chance of being a healthy adult later. You may go to physical education class several times a week, but you should also try to stay fit outside of school. You and your family can make healthy choices together. You can choose fresh fruit for dessert instead of cake. Offer to help make dinner one night, and surprise your family by preparing a delicious salad. You can go for a walk together after dinner instead of watching TV. Exercising can help wake up your brain so that you can do a good job on your homework. Making healthy choices may seem hard now, but it will feel good after a while.

1. What is the main idea of this passage?

    A. Going to physical education class is fun.

    B. Making healthy choices is too hard.

    C. Health and fitness are important for you and your family.

2. What might happen if you start good health habits now? _____

   _____

3. Where should you try to stay fit? _____

4. What can you do instead of watching TV after dinner? _____

   _____

Imagine you were selected to play on a major league baseball team. What position would you want to play? Write a journal entry about your first day on the team. Share it with your family members.

▶ **Draw a line to match each related division and multiplication problem.**

1.	65 ÷ 5	A.	9 × 4	9.	72 ÷ 9	I.	18 × 4
2.	24 ÷ 6	B.	6 × 4	10.	38 ÷ 2	J.	8 × 9
3.	36 ÷ 9	C.	9 × 5	11.	72 ÷ 4	K.	22 × 4
4.	45 ÷ 5	D.	17 × 3	12.	50 ÷ 2	L.	19 × 2
5.	28 ÷ 7	E.	7 × 4	13.	56 ÷ 4	M.	43 × 2
6.	64 ÷ 8	F.	9 × 9	14.	86 ÷ 2	N.	25 × 2
7.	51 ÷ 3	G.	8 × 8	15.	88 ÷ 4	O.	14 × 4
8.	81 ÷ 9	H.	13 × 5	16.	75 ÷ 3	P.	25 × 3

Design your own wrapping paper. Take a large sheet of paper and markers and create the wrapping paper. Then, share the design with your family.

American Education Publishing™

▶ **Circle each word that needs a capital letter.**

4407 ninth street

hillside, maine 04024

march 10, 2010

skateboards and more

6243 rock avenue

detroit, michigan 48201

To whom it may concern:

I am returning my skateboard for repair. it is still under warranty. please repair it and return the skateboard to the address above as soon as possible.

sincerely,

wesley diaz

You have a business that specializes in pet bathing services. You want more business. You decide a fun jingle will help promote your pet-bathing business. Write the jingle and then sing it for your family.

▶ **Congruent** figures have the same size and shape. Decide if each pair of figures is congruent. Circle the correct answer.

1.

congruent   not congruent

2.

congruent   not congruent

3.

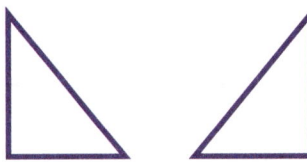

congruent   not congruent

4.

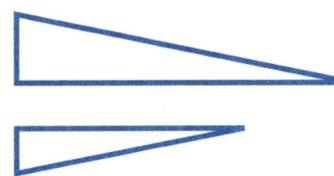

congruent   not congruent

Go to your bedroom. Look inside the dresser drawers. What do you see? Is there a drawer that needs to be organized? Well, start organizing it! Then, show the organized drawer to an adult family member. Is he impressed by your work?

▶ **Separate each run-on sentence into two sentences. Use correct capitalization and punctuation to write the new sentences.**

1. Raven has a new backpack it is green and has many zippers.

   _____

   _____

2. Katie borrowed my pencil she plans to draw a map.

   _____

   _____

3. Zoe is outside she is on the swings.

   _____

   _____

4. Zack is helping Dad Elroy is helping Dad too.

   _____

   _____

Post an ad letting your family members know you are available to help them around the house. Write the ad including what you are willing to do, such as wash dishes, fold laundry, sweep the floor, and so on. Make your ad no longer than 15 words. Post your ad and then see what response you get.

▶ **Circle the measurement from the parentheses that correctly completes each sentence.**

1. A bathtub could hold up to (10 quarts, 10 gallons) of water.

2. A flower vase could hold up to (1 liter, 1 milliliter) of water.

3. A bike would weigh (20 grams, 20 kilograms).

4. An orange would weigh (7 ounces, 7 pounds).

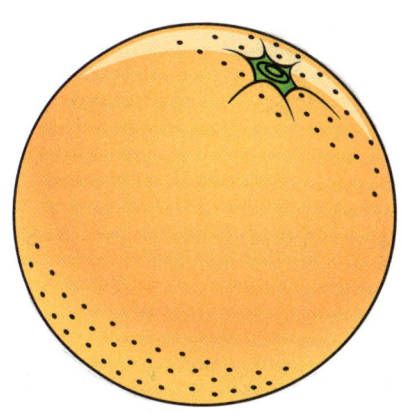

5. An ear of corn would be (11 inches, 11 yards) long.

6. A new pencil would be (7 meters, 7 centimeters) long.

Have a family member help you find pictures of yourself as a baby, as a kindergartener, and at your current age. Find a comfortable place to sit with the adult family member. Then, talk about the pictures, noting special memories and the changes you see.

American Education Publishing™

▶ **Underline the word from the parentheses that correctly completes each sentence.**

1. There aren't (no, **any**) letters for you today.

2. I don't (**ever**, never) get to go camping.

3. Hasn't (**anybody**, nobody) seen my green jacket?

4. Rob bumped his head; he doesn't remember (nothing, **anything**).

5. I (**haven't**, have) never flown in a jet.

6. I don't have (no, **any**) work to do.

7. There is never (**anything**, nothing) fun to do on Saturday.

8. Can't (nobody, **anybody**) fix this step?

Go to the park with an adult family member. Bring along some food scraps. Find an ant colony. Spill some food and observe what happens. Talk about what you see happening.

▶ **Read the story. Then, answer the questions.**

Sounds of Nature

Julie and Clint closed their eyes to shut out the sun's glare. As they sat on the ground, the hot July sun felt good. They could hear the wind blowing softly through the pine trees, making a kind of whispering, murmuring sound. They could hear the creek nearby making soothing, babbling sounds. They could even hear the distant screech of a hawk flying high in the sky overhead.

1. Where do you think Julie and Clint are? _____

2. What season of the year is it? _____

3. What could Julie and Clint hear? _____
   _____

4. What would you like to do if you were there? _____
   _____

You and a friend are going on a long bicycle ride. Where would be a good place to ride? Write a journal entry about your bicycle ride. Share it with your friends.

▶ **Imagine that you are having a party to celebrate something good. Write about what you are celebrating. Then, in the box below, design an invitation for your party.**

_____
_____
_____
_____
_____
_____
_____

Find out when and where a farmers' market happens in your city. Talk with an adult family member about scheduling a time to go. Mark the date on your calendar and then go. Be sure to take a shopping bag with you!

▶ **Read the story. Then, answer the questions.**

Swimming Lessons

Ann and her brother took swimming lessons this summer. Because they live in the country, they took a bus to the pool. It took half an hour to get there. Their lessons were two hours long, then they rode the bus home. Even though it took a lot of time, they enjoyed it very much. By the end of the summer, they both knew how to swim well.

1. What is the better summary for this story?

    A. Ann and her brother took swimming lessons this summer.

    B. Ann and her brother rode a bus to the pool to take swimming lessons this summer. They both enjoyed it and learned how to swim.

2. Should a summary be longer or shorter than the original story?

    _____

3. What information should be included in the summary?

    _____

    _____

    _____

Create a 30-second commercial for a company that makes sunglasses. Promote their sunglasses and why it is important to wear sunglasses. Use the Internet to research the importance of sunglasses. Write the commercial and then share it with friends and family.

▶ **Solve each word problem. Show your work.**

1. Don is picking apples. He puts 36 apples in each box. How many apples does he put in 9 boxes?

2. Tony is next to last in line. He is also 10th from the 1st person in line. How many people are in line?

3. Zack has saved $9.00 toward buying a new ball. He will get $3.00 today from his father. How much more money will he need to buy the $19.95 ball?

4. Jenna saves 867 pennies in May, 942 in July, and 716 in June. How many pennies does she save in these three months?

What if besides New Year's Eve, there was also a big celebration for Half-Year's Eve? Design a party invitation for a Half-Year's Eve party. Share your invitation with family members and friends. Are they ready to party with you on Half-Year's Eve?

▶ Read each group of words. Write *S* if it is a sentence, *F* if it is a fragment, or *R* if it is a run-on sentence.

1. _____ Orangutans are rare animals.

2. _____ Live in rain forests in Borneo and Sumatra.

3. _____ They belong to the ape family along with the chimpanzees and gorillas and they are larger than most chimpanzees and smaller than most gorillas.

4. _____ Approximately three to five feet tall.

5. _____ Their arms are extremely long.

Summer is a good time to wear a hat. Hats help protect you from harmful sun rays. Take an old catalog or magazine. Look for pictures of hats that you like. Cut out the pictures and create a hat collage. Share your collage with your family members.

▶ **Where would you find the answer to each of the following questions? Write the name of the best reference from the word bank.**

>   dictionary   globe   encyclopedia

1. Where is Oregon? _____

2. How do they harvest sugarcane in Hawaii? _____

3. Which syllable is stressed in the word *Utah*? _____

4. What kind of food do people eat in Mexico? _____

5. Which continent is closest to Australia? _____

6. Where is the Indian Ocean? _____

7. Who was Thomas Edison, and what did he do? _____

8. What does the word *hibernate* mean? _____

9. What are two different meanings for the word *project*? _____

Imagine you were just hired by a vegetable that wanted to be liked by your neighbors. Which vegetable would it be? Design a billboard sign with a message to your neighbors explaining why they should like the vegetable. Share your billboard design with family and friends.

▶ **Read the passage. Then, answer the questions.**

The History of Riddles

Riddles give a symbolic meaning to things. They have been used for thousands of years. In ancient times, wise people would often answer questions with riddles. It was believed that knowledge was **precious**, or of great value, and should not be given to everyone. If a person could solve a riddle, he was smart enough to know the answer.

1. What is the main idea of this passage?
    A. Riddles are used as symbols.
    B. Riddles have been used for many years.
    C. Riddles are hard to figure out.

2. The word **precious** means:
    A. a lot of money
    B. meaning
    C. valuable

3. What is a riddle?
   _____

4. Instead of giving an answer, why did wise people speak in riddles?
   _____

Keep your neighbors laughing. Start by making a list of 10 things that make you laugh. Share the list with family members and ask them to add to the list.

▶ **The proofreading mark ⌃ is used to show where a word, letter, or punctuation mark needs to be added in a sentence. Use the proofreading mark ⌃ to show where commas are needed in each sentence.**

1. As a bird of prey the American kestrel eats insects mice lizards and other birds.

2. Birds of prey such as hawks have hooked beaks and feet with claws.

3. Falcons are powerful fliers and they can swoop from great heights.

4. The American kestrel the smallest North American falcon is only 8 inches (20.3 cm) long.

5. "Kim, come look at this book about falcons."

Red, orange, yellow, green, blue, and purple: Which is your favorite color? Write a poem about your favorite color. Then, read it to family members and friends.

▶ **Read the passage. Then, answer the questions.**

Scientific Experiments

Scientists learn about the world by conducting experiments. They take careful notes about the supplies they use and the results they find. They share their findings with others, which leads to everyone learning a little more. You can do experiments too! The library has many books with safe experiments for students. You might work with balloons, water, or baking soda. You might learn about how light travels or why marbles roll down a ramp. Ask an adult to help you set up your experiment and to make sure that you are being safe. Be sure to wash your hands afterward and clean up the area. Take good notes about your work. Remember, you may be able to change just one thing the next time to get a completely different result. Most of all, do not worry if your results are different from what you expected. Some of the greatest scientific discoveries were made by mistake!

1. What is the main idea of this passage?
   A. Scientists learn about the world by conducting experiments.
   B. Scientists sometimes make mistakes that lead to great discoveries.
   C. You should always take good notes when conducting an experiment.

2. Why should you ask an adult to help you with your experiment?
   _____

3. Should you worry if you get different results? Why or why not?
   _____

Imagine your toothbrush and toothpaste could talk. What kind of early-morning conversation might they have with you? Make a four-panel comic strip that shows how your toothbrush and toothpaste might greet you each morning. Post your comic strip for family members to enjoy.

▶ **Solve each problem.**

1. 25 − 5 = _____
2. 36 − 16 = _____
3. 18 − 8 = _____
4. 28 ÷ 4 = _____
5. 36 ÷ 6 = _____
6. 9 × 2 = _____
7. 11 × 11 = _____
8. 16 + 6 = _____
9. 17 + 3 = _____
10. 6 × 1 = _____
11. 18 ÷ 3 = _____
12. 10 × 3 = _____
13. 14 ÷ 7 = _____
14. 5 × 6 = _____
15. 7 × 7 = _____
16. 42 ÷ 6 = _____

How many different ways can you find to fold napkins? Take 10 napkins and explore a different way to fold each one. Show the 10 folded napkins to your family members.

▶ **Read the passage. Then, follow the directions.**

Not Everyone Calls Them Pancakes

In France, pancakes are called crepes. They are made with flour, eggs, and other ingredients. They are usually rolled up with different kinds of food inside. Most often, they are filled with fruit. In Mexico, pancakes made with cornmeal are called tortillas. Tortillas are filled with a mixture of foods. Tortillas can also be folded to make tacos.

▶ **Below, write a recipe for your favorite pancakes. Describe what you like to have on top of them.**

_____

_____

_____

_____

_____

_____

_____

_____

Make a list of 20 animals that live in the zoo. Share your list with your family. Do they have any animals to add to the list?

▶ The range is the difference between the largest number and the smallest number in a group. To calculate the mean (or average), add all of the numbers, then divide by the number of items. The median is the middle number that appears in a group. The mode is the number that appears most often. Use the data to answer each question.

Lengths of Whales and Dolphins

Whales	Dolphins
blue whale..............................88 feet	bottle-nosed dolphin................9 feet
humpback whale ....54 feet	rough-toothed dolphin.............8 feet
gray whale..............................39 feet	Atlantic spotted dolphin...........7 feet
sperm whale ....35 feet	spinner dolphin........................7 feet
beluga whale ....13 feet	

1. What is the mean of the data? _____

2. What is the median of the data? _____

3. What is the mode of the data? _____

Make a plan to camp out overnight in your friend's yard. Make a list of what you will need to take with you. Share your overnight camp-out information with family members. Do they see anything to add to the list?

▶ Fill in the blanks with words that tell how a cat and dog are alike and different. The first ones have been done for you.

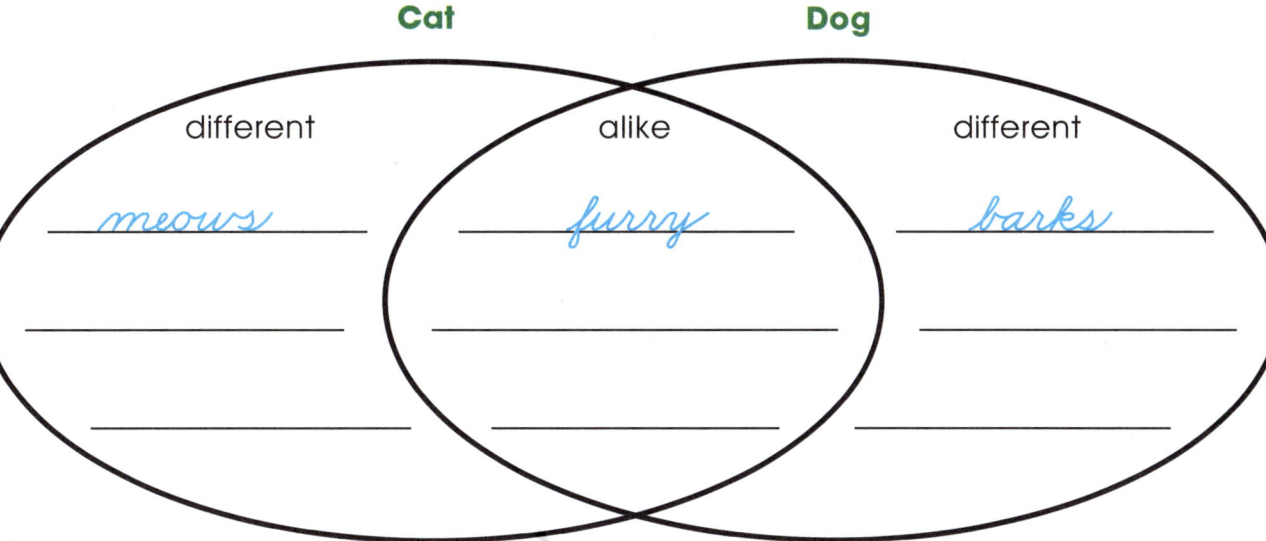

▶ Write two paragraphs below. In the first paragraph, tell how cats and dogs are alike. Tell how they are different in the second paragraph. Give each paragraph a title.

_____   _____

_____   _____

_____   _____

_____   _____

_____   _____

_____   _____

Find ways to encourage your family. Post an uplifting quotation on the refrigerator. Ask your adult family members for quote suggestions. Then, choose one and post it on the refrigerator.

▶ **Write the correct probability word from the word bank to complete each sentence.**

> certain   more likely   less likely   impossible

Pascal has 13 CDs in his CD case. Six CDs are rock, 2 CDs are hip-hop, 2 CDs are country, and 3 CDs are classical.

1. Pulling a classical CD from the case is _____ than pulling a rock CD from the case.

2. Pulling a rock CD from the case is _____ than pulling a country CD from the case.

3. Pulling a jazz CD from the case is _____ .

4. Pascal has another case of 16 CDs, and all 16 of the CDs are classical. Pulling a classical CD from the new case is _____ .

You were just selected to go on a trip to the moon! Write a journal entry telling about how you were selected and how you felt being selected to travel in space. Share your journal entry with your family members.

▶ **Complete the story web. Then, use the words in the web to write a story. Be sure to use proper punctuation. Think of a title for your story.**

Things to Think About

Who is this story about?

Where does this story take place?

How does this story begin?

What happens next?

How will this story end?

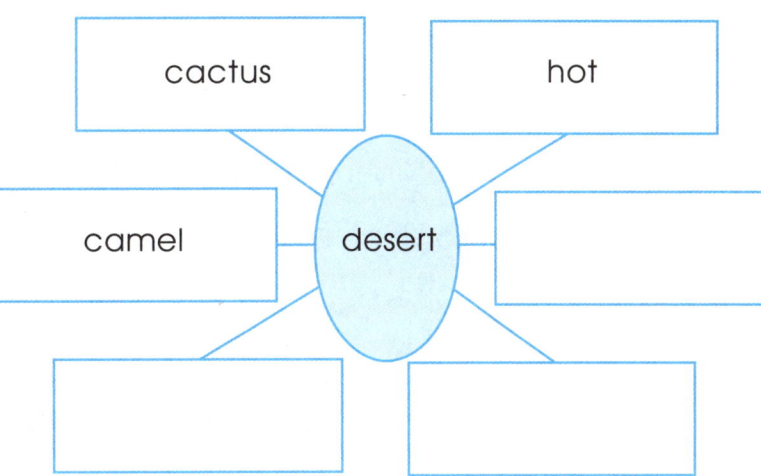

_____

_____

_____

_____

_____

_____

_____

Time to go on a shoe safari! Have a family member join you. Take paper and a pencil and search for shoes. Make a tally mark for each pair of shoes you find. How many pairs of shoes did you find? Share the results of the shoe safari with your family.

▶ **Adding commas between items in a series helps give meaning to a sentence. Write the letter of each correctly punctuated sentence.**

1. _____ Five children went on a bus to the zoo.

    A. Jeannie, Julio, John, Dennis, and Dave went together.

    B. Jeannie, Julio, John Dennis, and Dave went together.

2. _____ There are three things to eat for lunch today.

    A. We have chicken, sandwiches, carrot sticks, and soup.

    B. We have chicken sandwiches, carrot sticks, and soup.

3. _____ Ted can't find his four sisters.

    A. Mary Ellen, Shauna, Reese, and Lisa are hiding.

    B. Mary, Ellen, Shauna, Reese, and Lisa are hiding.

Choose a fairy tale. Then, rewrite it so that it is funny. Share the funny fairy tale with your family and friends.

▶ Read the passage. Then, answer the questions.

Flags

A flag tells something special about a country or a group. For example, the United States flag has 13 red and white stripes for the country's first 13 states. It has 50 white stars on a blue background to represent the current 50 states. The Canadian flag has a red maple leaf on a white background between two bands of red. The maple tree is the national tree of Canada. Canadian provinces and U.S. states also have their own flags. The state flag of Texas has a large white star on a blue background on the left and two bands of red and white on the right. The star symbolizes Texas's independence from Mexico. Because of the flag's single star, Texas is called the Lone Star State. The flag of the Canadian province New Brunswick has a gold lion on a red background above a sailing ship. The lion stands for ties to Brunswick, Germany, and to the British king. The ship represents the shipping industry.

1. What is the main idea of this passage?

    A. A flag tells something special about the country or the group it represents.

    B. Some flags have maple leaves or lions on them.

    C. Many flags are red, white, or blue.

2. What does the United States flag look like? _____
   _____

3. Why is Texas called the Lone Star State? _____
   _____

What if today were declared backwards day? Make a list of 10 things that you could do backwards. Share the list with family members. Do they have anything to add to the list?

▶ **Find out how many syllables are in each word by counting the number of vowels you hear when you say the word. Write the number on the blank.**

1. machine _____
2. somersault _____
3. peanut _____
4. neighborhood _____
5. astronaut _____
6. koala _____
7. dragon _____
8. itch _____
9. hero _____
10. auditorium _____
11. longitude _____
12. congratulate _____
13. frog _____
14. multiplication _____
15. Canada _____
16. zipper _____
17. gulf _____
18. lasagna _____

Brushing your teeth twice a day is good for you. It is also good to spend at least 60 seconds each time you brush. Place a timer near the bathroom sink. Talk with family members about timing themselves each time they brush their teeth.

▶ **How can the pitch of a sound be changed?**

Pitch is a property of sound. A sound's pitch is determined by the frequency of the waves that are producing it. Pitch is often described in terms of the highness or lowness of a sound.

Materials:
- 30 inches (76 cm) of string
- metal spoon
- table

Procedure:
Tie the handle of the spoon to the center of the string. Wrap the ends of the string around your index fingers.

Place the tip of each index finger in each ear. Lean over so that the spoon hangs freely. Tap the spoon against the side of a table. Listen carefully. Then, record your observations on the chart below.

Shorten the string by wrapping more of it around your fingers. Tap the spoon against the table again. Then, record your observations on the chart below.

Trial	Observations
1	
2	

What Is This All About?
The vibrating molecules in the spoon hit the string's molecules. The energy is transferred up the string to your ears. When the vibrations travel across a long string, they spread out and have a lower frequency and a lower pitch.

You are the chef of summertime fun. Design a poster showing yourself as a chef making a special summertime fun soup. What ingredients will you put in the soup? Share your poster with family and friends.

▶ **Haiku** is a form of Japanese poetry that follows a special pattern of 17 syllables. There are 5 syllables in the first line, 7 in the second line, and 5 in the third line. Most haiku poetry is about nature. Read the following haiku poem.

> Flakes of snow outside.
> Icicles hanging from eaves.
> Winter is here now.

▶ Use the lines to write a haiku poem of your own about apples, summer, or anything you want.

_____

_____

_____

You have a new title as "ruler" of your home! Take a ruler and measure different objects around the home. Make a list of the items you measure. Next to each item, write how tall or how long it is. Share the results with your family.

▶ **What conditions affect seeds as they germinate?**

Materials:
- 2 small, empty jars
- masking tape
- pencil
- scissors
- 10 radish seeds
- sheet of paper towel
- permanent marker
- water

Procedure:

Open one jar. Draw four circles on the paper towel, using the mouth of the jar as your guide. Cut out the circles.

Put one paper towel circle in the bottom of each jar. Then, put five radish seeds into each jar. Put another paper towel circle over the radish seeds in each jar. Each jar should now have a "sandwich" made of two paper towel circles and five radish seeds.

Add enough water to each jar to moisten, but not drown, the paper towel circles. If you add too much water, pour it out; the seeds will be OK. Label your jars with the pencil and the masking tape. Label one jar *warm* and the other *cold*.

Put the *cold* jar in the refrigerator. Put the *warm* jar in a warm, dark place where it will not be disturbed, such as a drawer. Check the seeds every day for four days. Record your observations on a separate sheet of paper.

In which location did the seeds germinate faster? Why do you think this is?

_____

_____

Create a mask using a paper plate. How will you turn the paper plate into a great-looking mask? Make a plan and then make the mask. Share the finished mask with family and friends.

▶ A product map uses symbols to show which products are produced in certain places. Below is a product map of Wisconsin. Study the map. Then, answer the questions.

1. What product does Wisconsin produce the most of? _____

2. Are more chickens or dairy cattle raised in Wisconsin? _____

3. Judging from the map, does Wisconsin produce more livestock or crops?
   _____

4. Why might it be helpful to know where products are produced?
   _____
   _____

Create a jingle for a company that makes and delivers pizzas. Write the jingle and then share it with friends and family members. Can you play an instrument to go with your jingle?

▶ **Read the passage. Then, answer the questions.**

Space Probes

We learn about planets by observing, or studying, them. Scientists use telescopes to see planets. A telescope is a special instrument that makes faraway objects look bigger. Some planets are too far away to see clearly, even when we use a telescope. How can we learn about these planets? Scientists send special spacecraft called probes into space. Telescopes and cameras are sent in the probe to record everything they see. Probes also carry special instruments to examine the weather and soil on other planets. The information is sent back to Earth where scientists can study it. The first probe, called Mariner 2, was launched in 1962. It gave us information about the planet Venus. Since then, scientists have sent over 25 probes into space. Each probe tells us even more about other planets.

1. What is the main idea of this passage?

    A. Probes tell us about other planets.

    B. Telescopes help us to see other planets.

    C. Mariner 2 was the first space probe.

2. What is a probe?

    _____

3. What information about other planets can a probe gather?

    _____

Design a garden that attracts butterflies and hummingbirds. Hummingbirds like red flowers. Butterflies like brightly colored flowers. Take paper and markers and create a garden where hummingbirds and butterflies are welcomed. Post your garden picture for your family to enjoy.

▶ **Use an atlas to make a map of Africa. Draw and label the features in the word bank. Then, follow the directions.**

Ahaggar Mountains	Lake Chad	Lake Victoria	Red Sea
Atlas Mountains	Madagascar (Island)	Namib Desert	Sahara Desert
Congo River	Lake Tanganyika	Nile River	Strait of Gibraltar
		Mediterranean Sea	

1. Color the deserts orange.
2. Draw brown triangles for the mountains.
3. Draw blue lines and circles for the rivers and lakes.
4. Draw a green line on the equator.
5. Draw red circles on the Tropic of Cancer and the Tropic of Capricorn.

Make a list of the rooms in your home. Take a pencil and paper and visit each room. Look at the floors and write what you see covering them: tile, carpet, or wood. After visiting each room, make a diagram of your home. Indicate on the diagram what is on the floor in each room. Share your diagram with family members.

▶ **Fill in the blanks with words that tell how a newspaper and a book are alike and different. The first ones have been done for you**

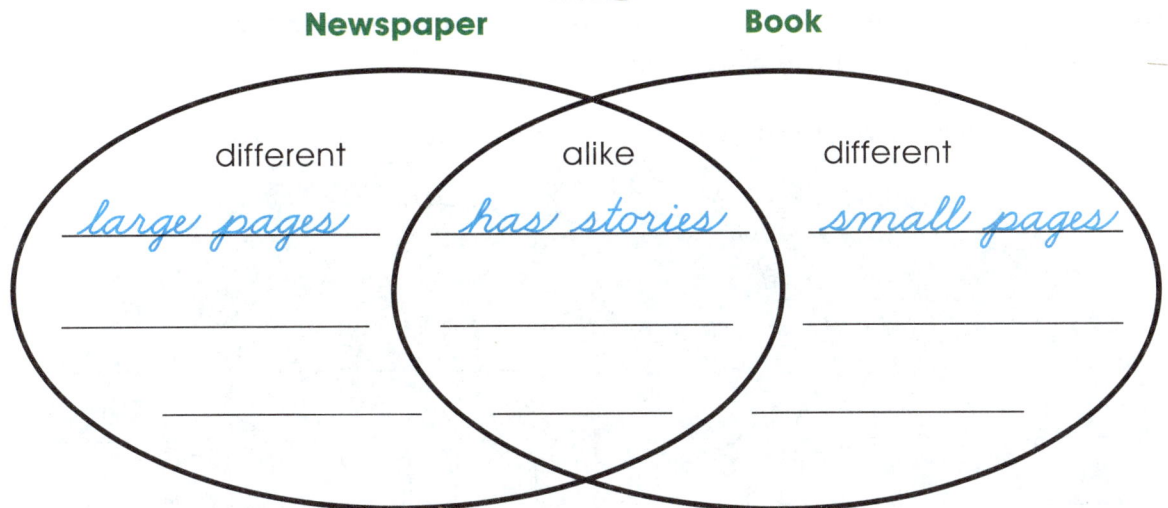

▶ **Write two paragraphs below. In the first paragraph, tell how newspapers and books are alike. Tell how they are different in the second paragraph. Give each paragraph a title.**

_____   _____
_____   _____
_____   _____
_____   _____
_____   _____
_____   _____

Promote a "turn off the lights" campaign at home. Look around your home, noting places where family members might need reminders to turn off the lights. At these places, post a fun reminder to turn off the lights.

▶ The prime meridian (0° longitude) and the meridian (180° longitude) divide Earth into two halves called the eastern hemisphere and the western hemisphere. Study the map below. Then, circle the correct hemisphere in parentheses to complete each sentence. Use an atlas or a world map if needed to help you identify each continent.

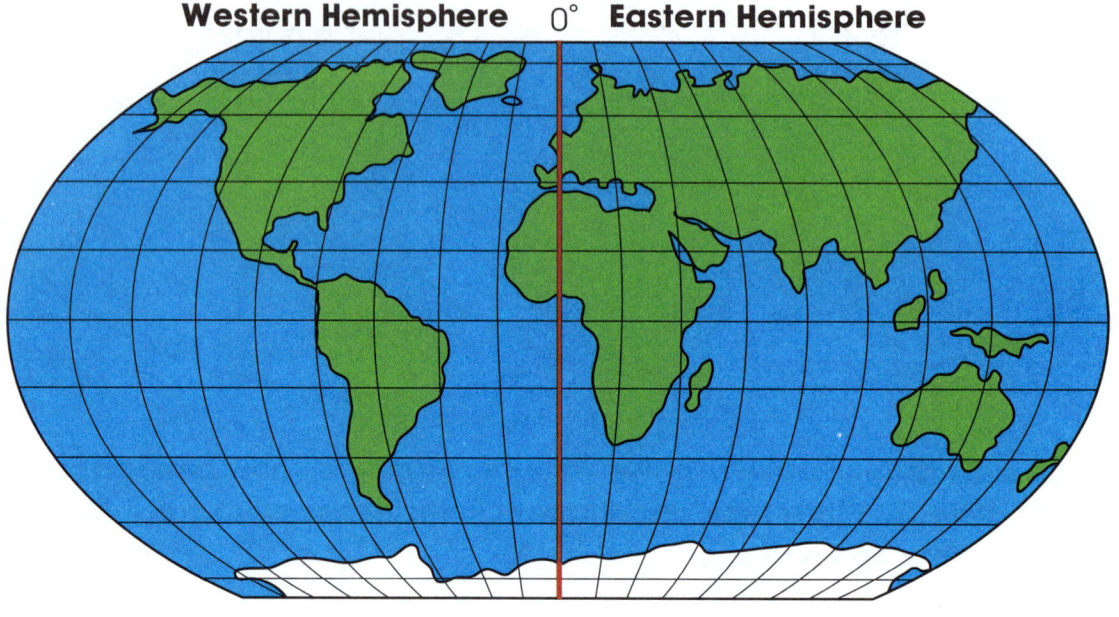

1. North America is in the (eastern, western) hemisphere.

2. Asia is mostly in the (eastern, western) hemisphere.

3. Africa is mostly in the (eastern, western) hemisphere.

4. South America is in the (eastern, western) hemisphere.

5. Europe is mostly in the (eastern, western) hemisphere.

6. Australia is in the (eastern, western) hemisphere.

Go for an animal observation walk around your neighborhood. Take a pencil and notebook with you. Write about what you observe the animals doing. Share your observations with your family.

▶ **Read each paragraph. Underline the sentence in each paragraph that does not belong.**

EXAMPLE:

Martha's dad is an electrician. He does many different kinds of things when he goes to work. Some days he checks the wiring in peoples' homes. Sometimes he checks the wiring in large buildings and shopping centers. <u>Martha is very proud of him.</u> He often helps put all the electrical wires and outlets in new buildings.

1. Jeremy has many reasons for wanting to be a dentist. He thinks having healthy teeth is very important. He has always been interested in all the things his own dentist does. Jeremy thinks he would be a good dentist too. <u>He has always enjoyed school.</u>

2. Being a florist takes special training. You must know the names of all the flowers and plants. <u>People who are in the hospital like to receive flowers.</u> You must learn how to care for flowers and plants. It is also important to know how to arrange them.

3. Carl wants to be a teacher, but he cannot decide what to teach. At first, he thought he would like to teach math. Then, he thought he would like to teach kindergarten. <u>Carl likes many things.</u> Now he thinks he would like to teach history.

Find a comfortable place to sit with an adult family member. Talk about recipes for making lemonade. Together, choose a recipe and then make some homemade lemonade.

▶ **Follow the directions below to learn more about nature.**

Take a notebook, a pencil, and a ruler outside. With an adult, find a garden or outdoor container garden where something is growing in groups, such as flowers, leaves, or vegetables. Locate the largest and smallest sample of each object and estimate their dimensions. Then, measure and compare each object. Continue estimating, measuring, and comparing objects until you are very close at estimating the exact answers.

You do not need a high-powered telescope to glimpse incredible sights in the night sky. With an adult, research the summer night sky to learn what stars can be seen where you live. Then, on a clear night, go outside with an adult. If you watch regularly, you might be able to see a meteor shower, a special star, or a distinctive constellation. Whatever the summer sky offers, keep a journal of your observations.

Archaeologists find and uncover objects. Then, they piece clues together to learn about the past. With your gardening gloves and a small shovel, go to an outdoor location where you have permission to dig. Dig several inches in a few different locations and examine what you find. Whether it is a quarter from 1978, an old button, or a fossil, you may be surprised by an interesting find. As you uncover the various items, consider how each object found its way into the earth. When you are finished, be sure to fill the holes you dug and clean up any mess that you made.

Imagine you just returned from a rainy camping trip with your family. Create a three-panel comic strip showing the adventures you had camping in the rain. Post your comic strip for family members to enjoy.

Answer Key

Page 1: 1. sums; 2. differences; 3. 10; 4. 48; 5. 69; 6. 35; 7. 2; 8. 27; 9. 16; 10. 46; 11. 58; 12. 12; 13. 29; 14. 69; 15. 11; 16. 12; 17. 56; 18. 23; 19. 39; 20. 78

Page 2: Students should follow directions.

Page 3: 1. B; 2. Glaciers form when snow hardens into ice over a long period of time; 3. Antarctica and Greenland; 4. There is a lot of snowfall in the winter and cool summers.

Page 4: 1. two; 2. read; 3. paws; 4. too; 5. too; 6. Red; 7. to; 8. pause

Page 5: 1–4.

5. SUMMER IS FUN

Page 6: 1. 8 + 7 = 15, 7 + 8 = 15, 15 - 8 = 7, 15 - 7 = 8; 2. 9 + 8 = 17, 8 + 9 = 17, 17 - 9 = 8, 17 - 8 = 9; 3. 6 + 8 = 14, 8 + 6 = 14, 14 - 6 = 8, 14 - 8 = 6

Page 7: Students should follow directions.

Page 8: 1. 902; 2. 1,476; 3. 770; 4. 1,133; 5. 1,031; 6. 1,223; 7. 890; 8. 880; 9. 601; 10. 1,201; 11. 405; 12. 1,223

Page 9: 1. D; 2. IN; 3. D; 4. D; 5. E; 6. E; 7. IM; 8. IN; 9. D; 10. E

Page 10: 1. dis-; 2. re-; 3. dis-; 4. un-; 5. in-; 6. in-; 7. dis-; 8. un-; 9. dis- or un-

Page 11: 1. nonfiction; Drawings will vary.

Page 12: 1. 16 books; 2. 8 photos; 3. 27 birds; 4. 5 tadpoles

Page 13: 1. S; 2. F; 3. F; 4. S; 5. F; 6. S; 7. S; 8. F; 9. S

Page 14: 1. 300 + 20 + 7, Students should draw 3 circles, 2 slashes, and 7 dots; 2. 254, Students should draw 2 circles, 5 slashes, and 4 dots; 3. 845, 800 + 40 + 5

Page 15: 1. large; 2. dried; 3. four; 4. good; 5. six; 6. many

Page 16: 1. F; 2. B; 3. NF; 4. F; 5. F; 6. B; 7. NF; 8. NF

Page 17: 1. 94; 2. 50; 3. 100; 4. 368; 5. 402; 6. 675; 7. 953; 8. 327

Page 18: 1. B; 2. Host countries get a chance to show their culture to athletes, visitors, and spectators.

Page 19: 1. 97; 2. 132; 3. 138; 4. 167; 5. 57; 6. 125; 7. 118; 8. 88; 9. 177

Page 20: 1. softer, softest; 2. larger, largest; 3. flatter, flattest; 4. sweeter, sweetest; 5. wider, widest; 6. cooler, coolest

Page 21: 1. 6.42; 2. 5.82; 3. 11.65; 4. 7.32; 5. 12.96; 6. 9.37; 7. 7.75; 8. 8.70; 9. 10.10; 10. 9.41; 11. 14.08; 12. 9.85

Page 22: 1–10. Answers will vary.

Page 23: No answer required.

Page 24: 1. Answers will vary but may include: 4 quarters, 10 dimes, 20 nickels, 100 pennies; 2. Answers will vary but may include: 1 quarter, 2 dimes and 1 nickel, 5 nickels, 1 dime and 15 pennies; 3. Answers will vary but may include: 16 dimes, 6 quarters and 1 dime, 32 nickels.

Page 25: 1–4. Answer will vary.; 5. This or That; 6. this or that; 7. That; 8. Those

Page 26: 1. 561; 2. 800; 3. 486; 4. 150; 5. 221; 6. 411

Page 27: 1. pineapple; 2. scarecrow; 3. snowstorm; 4. horseback; 5. teammates

Page 28: 1. 90; 2. 10; 3. 40; 4. 30; 5. 90; 6. 80; 7. 20; 8. 800; 9. 200; 10. 800; 11. 600

Page 29: 1. cousin, Spain; 2. bear, Smokey; 3. family, Pizza Barn; 4. city, Ogden; 5. scientist, Isaac Newton; 6. satellite, Sputnik I; 7. cameras, George Eastman; 8. months, Pilgrims

American Education Publishing™

Answer Key (continued)

Page 30: Last summer, we went camping in Colorado. We went hiking and swimming every day. One time, I actually saw a baby white-tailed deer with spots. We also took photos of a lot of pretty rocks, flowers, and leaves. We had a great time! I didn't want to leave.

Page 31: 1. 132; 2. 107; 3. 75; 4. 195; 5. 166; 6. 109; 7. 146; 8. 122; 9. 151; 10. 126; 11. 113; 12. 99

Page 32: 1. <u>nowhere</u>, anywhere; 2. <u>nobody</u>, anybody or somebody; 3. <u>no</u>, any; 4. <u>never</u>, ever; 5. <u>nothing</u>, anything

Page 33: 1. 561, 656, 683, 6,283; 2. 411, 882, 8,311, 8,899; 3. 642, 742, 6,420, 7,420; 4. 444, 4,000, 4,040, 4,444; 5. 7,138, 3,778, 737, 397; 6. 9,998, 9,989, 998, 899; 7. 6,487, 786, 472, 242; 8. 6,565, 5,565, 665, 565

Page 34: Students should circle the following words: elephant, tent, Mr. Chip, team, book, California, guitar, Lake Street, Kent, strength, engine, broccoli; Students should underline the following words: sang, ate, fixed, laugh, landed, cleaned, yell, played, visited, write, jump, leap.

Page 35: 1. cac/tus; 2. blis/ter; 3. al/ways; 4. har/bor; 5. flow/er; 6. bas/ket; 7. o/beys

Page 36: 1. <; 2. <; 3. <; 4. >; 5. =; 6. >; 7. <; 8. <

Page 37: 1. 2; 2. 1; 3. 2; 4. 3; 5. 2; 6. 1; 7. 4; 8. 1

Page 38: 1. <; 2. >; 3. <; 4. >; 5. <; 6. <; 7. <; 8. <; 9. >; 10. >; 11. <; 12. <

Page 39: 1. tip; 2. lid; 3. happy; 4. tear; 5. tug; 6. silent; 7. mistake; 8. small

Page 40: 1 Wed.; 2. Jan.; 3. Aug.; 4. Sun.; 5. Thurs.; 6. Feb.; 7. Sept.; 8. Mon.; 9. Fri.; 10. Mar.; 11. Oct.; 12. Tues.; 13. Sat.; 14. Apr.; 15. Nov.

Page 41: A. 57; B. 99; C. 81; D. 83; E. 13; F. 75; G. 84; H. 81; I. 42; 1. 57 < 84; 2. 81 = 81, 3. 99 > 42; 4. 75 > 13; 5. 83 < 84; 6. 13 < 81

Page 42: 1. C; 2. It was the network of people who helped slaves escape to safety; 3. They helped slaves move to freedom.

Page 43: 1. 642; 2. 582; 3. 1,165; 4. 732; 5. 1,296; 6. 937; 7. 775; 8. 870; 9. 1,010; 10. 1,083; 11. 791; 12. 1,071

Page 44: 1. Dogs, cats, gerbils, and hamsters can be pets; 2. I am wearing blue jeans, a striped shirt, black shoes, green socks, and a baseball cap.

Page 45: 1. rectangle; 2. hexagon; 3. pentagon; 4. octagon; 5. square; 6. triangle

Page 46: Students should draw three lines under the first letter of each of the following words: pocahontas, virginia, english, america, pocahontas, captain, john, smith, jamestown, rebecca, mr., john, rolfe, england, king, james, pocahontas, england, thomas.

Page 47: 1. numb; 2. knead; 3. certain; 4. purchase; 5. sense; 6. wheat; 7. guide; 8. praise

Page 48: No answer required.

Page 49: 1. 1,033; 2. 1,333; 3. 1,324; 4. 1,164; 5. 1,610; 6. 1,133; 7. 1,272; 8. 783; 9. 601; 10. 842; 11. 1,010; 12. 1,001

Page 50: Students should draw three lines under the first letter of each of the following words: july, dear, aunt, i've, uncle, your.

Page 51: 1. 586; 2. 582; 3. 1,382; 4. 1,441; 5. 1,207; 6. 1,060; 7. 1,007; 8. 974; 9. 1,089; 10. 1,062; 11. 945; 12. 786

Page 52: 1. My parents were married in Portland, Oregon, on May 1, 1999. 2. We had chicken, potatoes, corn, gravy, and ice cream for dinner. 3. George Washington became the first U. S. president on April 30, 1789. 4. Sam was born on June 16, 1947, in Rome, Italy. 5. We saw deer, bears, elk, and goats on our trip. 6. On July 24, 1962, in Boise, Idaho, I won the big race.

Page 53: 1–6. Answers will vary.

Page 54: Students should circle the first letters of the following words: today, i, i, wednesday, april, billings, montana, my, mom, dad, my, david, rose, after, grandma, grandpa, we, they, happy, birthday, then; i; Answers will vary.

Page 55: 1. equal to; 2. more than; 3. less than; 4. equal to; 5. less than; 6. equal to; 7. more than; 8. equal to

Answer Key (continued)

Page 56: 1. knock; 2. hopped; 3. night; 4. numb; 5. different; 6. dry

Page 57: 1. A; 2. an earthquake hit; 3. to deliver supplies to help people after the earthquake

Page 58: 1. 9; 2. 12; 3. June 29; 4. 15

Page 59: Students should circle the following: 1. We; 2. A little red fox; 3. Some birds; 4. Clowns; 5. The king; 6. April; 7. Lee; 8. We; 9. The frog; 10. Lions; 11. Olivia's mom; 12. Noah; 13. I; 14. Mom and I; Students should underline the following: 1. went on a picnic; 2. ran past us; 3. make nests for their eggs; 4. make me laugh; 5. rode a bike; 6. lost her house keys; 7. auditioned for the school play; 8. started to swim; 9. hopped onto the lily pad; 10. live in groups called prides; 11. baked the pie; 12. worked in his garden; 13. finished the book yesterday; 14. rode our horses.

Page 60: 1. 43; 2. 9; 3. 7; 4. 54; 5. 13; 6. 10; 7. 29; 8. 7; 9. 18; 10. 39; 11. 18; 12. 7

Page 61: 1. is; 2. are; 3. am; 4. are; 5. am; 6. are; 7. is

Page 62: 1. 7 tubes; 2. 14 baskets; 3. 3 teachers; 4. 8 tickets

Page 63: 1. jazz, The other words are all instruments; 2. tire, The other words are all tools; 3. dog, The other words are all birds; 4. moon, The other words are all planets; 5. peach, The other words are all vegetables; 6. lazy, The other words are all flowers.

Page 64: 1. 7; 2. 14; 3. 47; 4. 29; 5. 18; 6. 49; 7. 19; 8. 66; 9. 46; 10. 15; 11. 57; 12. 8

Page 65: 1. will cook; 2. will visit; 3. will go; 4. will read; 5. will show

Page 66: 1. 3.66; 2. 14.76; 3. 2.16; 4. 11.64; 5. 4.33; 6. 12.23; 7. 8.90; 8. 2.34; 9. 6.01; 10. 3.08; 11. 5.84; 12. 2.27

Page 67: 1. saddest; 2. action; 3. direction; 4. safest or safety; 5. dirty or dirtiest; 6. hungriest; 7. invention; 8. preparation; 9. happiest; 10. honesty

Page 68: 1. 6.26; 2. 2.40; 3. 2.44; 4. 11.52; 5. 413; 6. 797; 7. 933; 8. 9; 9. 100; 10. 2.17; 11. 942; 12. 636

Page 69: 1. are; 2. is; 3. are; 4. is; 5. is; 6. are; 7. is; 8. are

Page 70: 1. 170; 2. 260; 3. 641; 4. 243; 5. 262; 6. 366; 7. 67; 8. 744; 9. 138; 10. 152; 11. 293; 12. 171

Page 71: No answer required.

Page 72: 1. 547, 496, 325, 261; 2. 793, 779, 746, 733; 3. 596, 579, 499, 488; 4. 964, 946, 649, 496; 5. 647, 674, 746, 764; 6. 353, 503, 530, 550; 7. 488, 499, 579, 940; 8. 496, 649, 946, 964

Page 73: 1. Jack was getting his picture taken; 2. special stool, camera, mother fussing; 3. "not comfortable," "Jack frowned," "He did not feel like smiling."

Page 74: 1. 0.59; 2. 1.64; 3. 0.89; 4. 3.08; 5. 4.49; 6. 4.89; 7. 1.81; 8. 0.37; 9. 3.89; 10. 0.14; 11. 6.79; 12. 1.79

Page 75: Answers will vary, but should include details from the story in order, such as: 1. Quinn and Phillip filled a bucket with soapy water; 2. They put soapy water all over the car and wiped off the dirt; 3. They rinsed the car with water and dried it with clean towels; 4. They were surprised when their dad gave them $5 each.

Page 76: 1. 123.34; 2. 139.58; 3. 78.86; 4. 128.57; 5. 145.63; 6. 111.15; 7. 129.52; 8. 96.71; 9. 84.91

Page 77: Students should circle the following: 1. (est), sad; 2. (est), hungry; 3. (tion), prepare; 4. (tion), invent; 5. (ty), taste; 6. (ty), certain; 7. (ty), loyal; 8. (tion), direct; 9. (est), lovely; 10. (est), sure

Page 78: 1. 375; 2. 1,306; 3. 1,213; 4. 1,031; 5. 3,913; 6. 9,235; 7. 8,390; 8. 7,258; 9. 10,237

Page 79: 1. C; 2. the main character in *Anne of Green Gables*; 3. She lived with her grandparents and went to school in a one-room schoolhouse; 4. Many people still visit Prince Edward Island today to see where Anne Shirley grew up.

Page 80: 1. 17,024; 2. 15,255; 3. 10,990; 4. 188; 5. 125; 6. 1,948; 7. 15,807; 8. 2,061; 9. 17,066

Page 81: 1. hatched; 2. looked; 3. used; 4. breathed; 5. changed; 6. started; 7. flattened; 8. vanished; 9. disappeared; 10. hopped

Answer Key (continued)

Page 82: 1–4. Answers will vary; 5. first, last

Page 83: 1. 13,011; 2. 1,410; 3. 166; 4. 1,350; 5. 239; 6. 180; 7. 1,305; 8. 12,077; 9. 24,672

Page 84: 1. planes; 2. hippo; 3. sub; 4. phone; 5. photo

Page 85: 1. 14,485; 2. 17,723; 3. 2,074; 4. 15,908; 5. 7,658; 6. 1,244; 7. 18,621; 8. 19,739; 9. 15,878

Page 86: 1. C; 2. the ropes sometimes broke; 3. the spring pulled the elevator up if the cables broke; 4. The New York Crystal Palace Exhibition in 1853

Page 87: Answers will vary.

Page 88: 1. L; 2. A; 3. L; 4. A; 5. A; 6. A; 7. L; 8. A; 9. A; 10. A; 11. L; 12. L; 13. A; 14. L

Page 89: 1. 10,368; 2. 5,392; 3. 11,742; 4. 36; 5. 226; 6. 312; 7. 2,688; 8. 3,589; 9. 2,835

Page 90: 1. B; 2. B; 3. A; 4. A; 5. B

Page 91: 1. 394; 2. 663; 3. 258; 4. 28; 5. 226; 6. 312; 7. 2,688; 8. 3,589; 9. 2,835

Page 92: Drawings will vary.

Page 93: 1. The ink spread up the coffee filter strips; 2. The inks separated into different colors.

Page 94: 1. 3,418; 2. 1,086; 3. 3,078; 4. 4,696; 5. 2,228; 6. 8,600; 7. 2,271; 8. 6,323; 9. 676

Page 95: 1. The higher the ramp, the faster the object moved; 2. Answers will vary.

Page 96: 1. 8, 16, 12, 18, 14; 2. 21, 15, 6, 12, 24; 3. 40, 32, 16, 28, 24, 36; 4. 45, 10, 30, 25, 35, 20

Page 97: 1. 0°; 2. W; 3. E; 4. Students should trace the prime meridian (0°) in orange on the map.

Page 98: 1. yes; 2. yes; 3. no; 4. no; 5. yes; 6. no; 7. yes; 8. yes; 9. yes; 10. yes

Page 99: 1. 60 miles; 2. 75 miles; 3. 30 miles; 4. 45 miles

Page 100: 1. 89; 2. 160; 3. 146; 4. 929; 5. 3,987; 6. 741; 7. 11,487; 8. 97,996; 9. 9,531; 10. 10,419; 11. 107,927; 12. 55,573

Page 101: 1. E; 2. H; 3. F; 4. J; 5. C; 6. D; 7. G; 8. A; 9. B; 10. I

Page 102: Answers will vary.

Page 103: No answer required.

Page 104: 1. Fulton; 2. Greenville; 3. Rocky Glen; 4. Capital City; 5. Eagle Nest; 6. Ocean City

Page 105: Answers will vary.

Page 106: Answers will vary.

Page 107: 1. "Where is the big beach ball?" asked Jeff.; 2. Ilene exclaimed, "That is a wonderful idea!"; 3. "Come and do your work," Grandma said, "or you can't go with us."; 4. "Yesterday," said Ella, "I saw a pretty robin in the tree by my window."; 5. "I will always take care of my pets," promised Theodore.; 6. Rachel said, "Maybe we should have practiced more."; 7. Dr. Jacobs asked, "How are you, Pat?"

Page 108: 1. 80; 2. 105; 3. 84; 4. 96; 5. 104; 6. 94; 7. 76; 8. 95; 9. 76

Page 109: Answers will vary.

Page 110: 1. 312; 2. 1,617; 3. 2,436; 4. 2,142; 5. 7,332; 6. 2,592; 7. 414; 8. 2,035; 9. 1,798

Page 111: Students should write the following words under *Common Nouns*: dog, boat, holiday, beans, Ocean, apple; Students should write the following words under *Proper Nouns*: November, Monday, Mr. Brown, Rex, Main Street, July.

Page 112: 1. B; 2. C

Page 113: 1. 300; 2. 240; 3. 1,112; 4. 987; 5. 2,110; 6. 2,820; 7. 7,443; 8. 6,482; 9. 3,260

Page 114: 1. two; 2. cent; 3. to; 4. sent; 5. too; 6. scent

Page 115: 1. Students should circle 5 groups of 3 squares each, 3; 2. Students should circle 2 groups of 8 pentagons each, 8; 3. Students should circle 4 groups of 2 triangles each, 2.

Page 116: 1. a, bed; 2. The, movie; 3. an, umbrella; 4. a, leak; 5. the, sun, the, rain; 6. an, apple, a, sandwich; 7. the, nails, an, egg carton; 8. The, books, the, shelf; 9. a, blue whale, the, ocean; 10. The, elephant

Answer Key (continued)

Page 117: 1. wonderful; 2. warm; 3. worried; 4. who; 5. where; 6. weigh; 7. want; 8. won't

Page 118: 1. 42; 2. 31; 3. 34; 4. 31; 5. 10; 6. 11; 7. 23; 8. 11; 9. 12; 10. 10; 11. 11; 12. 20

Page 119: No answer required.

Page 120: 1. 6; 2. 5; 3. 12; 4. 9; 5. 7; 6. 5; 7. 8; 8. 4; 9. 9; 10. 9; 11. 4; 12. 8

Page 121: Answers will vary.

Page 122: 1. pears; 2. seem; 3. flour; 4. right; 5. won; 6. dough

Page 123: 1. the diamond; 2. (2,2); 3. Students should circle the triangle; 4. Students should draw a line between the rectangle and the circle; 5. the circle

Page 124: 1. bear, bare; 2. vain, vein; 3. dew, due; 4. tee, tea; 5. weight, wait; 6. hair, hare

Page 125: 1. 3:30; 2. 55 minutes; 3. 4:00; 4. 3:45

Page 126: 1. the; 2. an; 3. a, a; 4. the; 5. the or a; 6. a; 7. the; 8. a

Page 127: 1. B; 2. A; 3. C; 4. C; 5. A

Page 128:
1. AB = Ray AB; 2. GH = Line GH (or HG); 3. LM = Line Segment LM (or ML); 4. CD = Line CD (or DC); 5. UT = Ray UT; 6. WX = Ray WX

Page 129:
1. usually, go; 2. slowly, drive; 3. often, begins; 4. loudly, plays; 5. excitedly, cheers; 6. near, pass; 7. beautifully, are decorated; 8. never, see

Page 130: 1. pictures; 2. market; 3. cottage; 4. quarter; 5. pennies; 6. circus; 7. bell; 8. curtains

Page 131: 1. read; 2. knew; 3. told; 4. said; 5. heard; 6. bought; 7. found; 8. ate

Page 132:

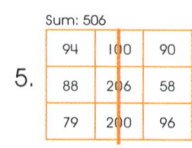
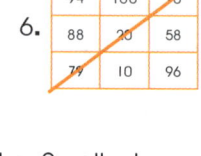

Page 133: 1. make; 2. rolled; 3. enjoyed; 4. helped or helps; 5. places or placed; 6. painted; 7. give or gave

Page 134: 1. A; 2. B; 3. B; 4. A

Page 135: 1. I rode down the hill on a bike.; 2. My mom and I planted a garden in our backyard.; 3. All of the animals braced themselves when the elephant sneezed.; 4. Cory pulled a wagon full of bottles.; 5. I closed my book and went to bed.

Page 136: 1. 15, 18, 21, 27; 2. 30, 36, 42, 54, 60; 3. 28, 32, 36, 40, 48; 4. 21, 18, 15, 12, 6; 5. 92, 90, 88, 84, 82

Page 137: 1. C; 2. clothing, bedding, and wall hangings; 3. caterpillar, cocoon, pupa, moth; 4. B

Page 138: 1. 60; 2. 20; 3. 10; 4. −10; 5. 5; 6. 30

Page 139: 1–2. Answers will vary.

Page 140: 1. 6; 2. 2, 3; 3. 2, 4

Page 141: 1. possible; 2. impossible; 3. possible; 4. certain; 5. possible; 6. certain

Page 142: 1. 8; 2. 8; 3. 7; 4. 1; 5. 5; 6. 9; 7. 4; 8. 7; 9. 3; 10. 4; 11. 11; 12. 2

Page 143: No answer required.

Page 144: 1. 3; 2. 2; 3. 5; 4. 3; 5. 4; 6. 4; 7. 5; 8. 6

Page 145: 1. correct; 2. correct; 3. careful; 4. correct; 5. garden; 6. babies; 7. correct; 8. correct; 9. movie; 10. correct

Page 146: 1. Robert loans his skateboard to his friend, and he can be counted on; 2. She is fair because she takes turns; 3. They ride bikes, go to school and camp together, and skateboard together.

Page 147: 1. 117 pounds; 2. 272 marbles; 3. 122 balls; 4. 7 cards

Page 148: 1–4. Answers will vary.

Answer Key (continued)

Page 149: 1. sang; 2. told; 3. brought; 4. worn; 5. took

Page 150: 1. D; 2. C

Page 151: 1. wolves; 2. shelves; 3. hooves; 4. children; 5. wives; 6. leaves

Page 152:

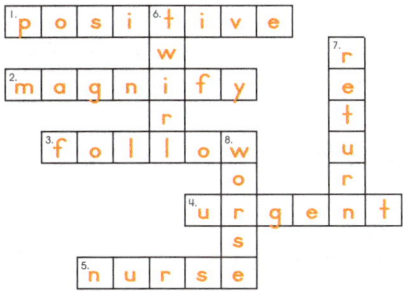

Page 153: 1. teachers; 2. potatoes; 3. houses; 4. kites; 5. classes; 6. clowns; 7. boxes; 8. handbooks; 9. watches; 10. friends; 11. clocks; 12. computers; 13. couches; 14. caramels

Page 154: 1. I; 2. E; 3. B; 4. C; 5. D; 6. A; 7. H; 8. F; 9. G

Page 155: 1. bear; 2. toe; 3. sail; 4. pale; 5. know; 6. sent; 7. male; 8. flower

Page 156: 1–2. Answers will vary.

Page 157: 1. Dana's; 2. Craig's; 3. Sharon's 4. children's; 5. girls'; 6. school's; 7. truck's; 8. actor's; 9. grandmother's; 10. singers'; 11. dogs'

Page 158:

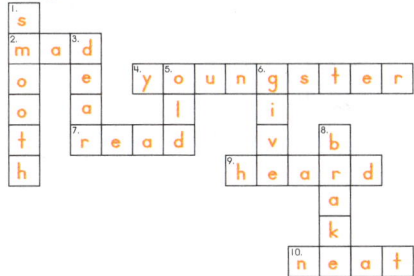

Page 159: 1. obtuse; 2. acute; 3. obtuse; 4. right

Page 160: 1. we're; 2. weren't; 3. wasn't; 4. wouldn't; 5. they have; 6. they will (or shall); 7. should not; 8. I would (or had)

Page 161: 1. o, o, u; 2. o, o, i, e; 3. o, a, e; 4. u, e, a; 5. o, o, i, e; 6. e, e

Page 162: 1. B; 2. empty the package into a microwave-safe bowl; 3. a package of oatmeal, microwave-safe bowl, measuring cup, water, microwave, milk, and spoon; 4. B

Page 163: 1. re; 2. un; 3. re; 4. un; 5. re

Page 164: 1. goeing, going; 2. cleen, clean; 3. baught, bought; 4. payed, paid; 5. snease, sneeze; 6. creem, cream; 7. frendly, friendly

Page 165: 1–5. Answers will vary.

Page 166: 1. He; 2. us; 3. I; 4. she; 5. they

Page 167: 1. Writing a Story; 2. 40; 3. 57

Page 168: Line 1. breakfast; Line 2. backpack; Line 3. classroom; Line 4. playground; Line 5. homework

Page 169: 1. 45 seeds; 2. 18 nickels; 3. $20.90; 4. 61 children

Page 170: 1. base word; 2. suffix; 3. prefix; 4. prefix; 5. base word; 6. suffix; 7. suffix; 8. prefix; 9. suffix; 10. base word; 11. base word; 12. base word; 13. suffix; 14. suffix;

15. prefix; 16. base word; 17. prefix; 18. suffix

Page 171: Answers will vary.

Page 172: 1. apple; 2. strawberry; 3. (1,1); 4. Students should draw a square around the grapes; 5. Students should circle the pineapple; 6. Students should draw a peach at (5,3).

Page 273: 1–6. Answers will vary.

Page 174: 1. $1.46; 2. $3.55; 3. $0.93; 4. $1.66

Page 175: 1. Penny's dog Coco likes to eat special snacks. 2. Oliver Owl is teaching Owen Owl to fly.

Page 176: 1. yes; 2. no; 3. no; 4. yes; 5. yes; 6. no; 7. no; 8. yes; 9. yes; 10. yes

Page 177: Answers will vary.

Page 178: Answers will vary.

Page 179: 1. cm; 2. m; 3. cm, cm; 4. km; 5. km; 6. m; 7. m; 8. km

Page 180: 1. umbrella; 2. Juan; 3. Amira and Becca; 4. Rachel; 5. toy; 6. bus

Page 181: 1. 4; 2. 8

Page 182: Answers may vary. Here is a sample of how the story can be completed: Angelica decided to write a book. She loved to read, and her teachers said that she had a great imagination. Her heroine would have green eyes and long, dark hair, just like Angelica. She would live in the middle of a deep,

Answer Key (continued)

vast forest. Angelica imagined the animals that might come to visit her character: tall bears, slender deer, and tiny mice. She worked on her story every day at lunchtime and after school. It grew longer and soon took up a whole notebook! Angelica let her best friend, Isabel, read her story. Isabel thought it was brilliant and very creative. She said she could not wait until Angelica was a famous author one day!

Page 183: 1. 5 x 3 = 15; 2. 7 x 4 = 28; 3. 5 x 1 = 5; 2 x 3 = 6

Page 184: 1. Answers will vary but should be fruits; 2. Answers will vary but should be utensils for eating; 3. Answers will vary but should be bodies of water; 4. Answers will vary but should be related to trees and wood; 5. Answers will vary but should be beverages; 6. Answers will vary but should be types of money; 7. Answers will vary but should be vegetables; 8. Answers will vary but should be articles of clothing; 9. Answers will vary but should be sports.

Page 185: 1. 2; 2. 5; 3. 4; 4. 6; 5. 2; 6. 2; 7. 1; 8. 1; 9. 3; 10. 9; 11. 7; 12. 9; 13. 7; 14. 5; 15. 7; 16. 2; 17. 6; 18. 8

Page 186: Line 1. Earth; Line 2. plant; Line 3. Plants, oxygen; Line 4. sunlight; Line 5. heat

Page 187: 1. 168 cakes; 2. about 250 gift baskets; 3. 42 souvenirs; 4. about 2,800 bags of popcorn, but answers may vary.

Page 188: 1. error; 2. afraid; 3. sofa; 4. present; 5. connect; 6. finish; 7. jewel; 8. cent; 9. alter

Page 189: 1. 12; 2. 42; 3. 12; 4. 55; 5. 36; 6. 91; 7. 32; 8. 28; 9. 10; 10. 566; 11. 54; 12. 570

Page 190: Line 1. weekends; Line 2. outside; Line 3. doghouse; Line 4. backyard; Line 5. butterfly; Line 6. nighttime

Page 191: Students should circle the following: 1. 4-point star; 2. pentagon

Page 192: Students should write the following words under *Compound Words*: buttermilk, snowstorm, daylight, airplane, football; Students should write the following words under *Words with Prefixes or Suffixes*: replanted, peaceful, selection, sleepless, unpacked

Page 193: 1. A; 2. A lot of rain falls quickly, filling the streets faster than water can drain; 3. Listen to TV or radio news reports and be ready to leave; 4. Listen to news reports so you know when it's safe to return home and drink tap water.

Page 194:

1. 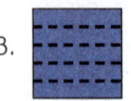 2.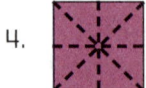

3.  4.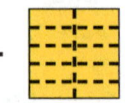

5. 6.

Page 195: 1. weightless; 2. thoughtful; 3. appointment

Page 196: Answers will vary.

Page 197: 1. >; 2. >; 3. <; 4. <; 5. <; 6. =; 7. =; 8. >; 9. <

Page 198: 1. B; 2. D; 3. A; 4. A

Page 199: 1. 0; 2. N; 3. S; Students should draw a red line across the map at the equator (0° latitude).

Page 200: 1. 5:10; 2. 1:40; 3. 10:42; 4. 4:25; 5. 4:10; 6. 4:55; 7. 5:20

Page 201: 1. D; 2. B; 3. A; 4. D

Page 202: 1. Calgary; 2. Denver; 3. Boston; 4. Charleston; 5. Montreal; 6. Salt Lake City; 7. San Francisco

Page 203: 1. Students should circle clock that is set at 8:30; 2 Students should circle digital clock that says 3:15; 3. Students should circle clock that says 6:45; 4. Students should circle clock that says 4:15.

Page 204: Drawings will vary.

Page 205: 1. 750 tires; 2. 2,250 tires

Page 206: Answers will vary.

Page 207: 1. $2.77; 2. $1.50; 3. $23.00

Page 208: 1. B; 2. A; 3. C; 4. C; 5. D

Page 209: 1–2. Answers will vary.

Page 210: 1. $2.50; 2. $0.05; 3. $0.20; 4. $3.58; 5. $10.65; 6. $0.45; 7. $6.05; 8. $15.00

Answer Key (continued)

Page 211: 1. play; 2. interest; 3. write; 4. cover; 5. spoon; 6. quick; 7. happy; 8. doubt; 9. kind; 10. cover

Page 212: 1. Chocolate, hot, chocolate, big, sticky, yummy, chocolate; 2. sunny, white, frightened, soft, sweet, big, happy, small

Page 213: 1. A; 2. A food web is a drawing that shows how living things are connected; 3. The animals who eat plants would not have as much food, and neither would the animals who eat those small animals, so there would be fewer of each type of animal.

Page 214: 1. 10; 2. 24; 3. 2; 4. 4; 5. 2; 6. 20; 7. 4; 8. 12

Page 215: 1. D; 2. B; 3. C; 4. B

Page 216: No answer required.

Page 217: 1. 5 x 3 = 15, 3 x 5 = 15, 15 ÷ 3 = 5, 15 ÷ 5 = 3; 2. 21 ÷ 3 = 7, 21 ÷ 7 = 3, 3 x 7 = 21, 7 x 3 = 21; 3. 30 ÷ 6 = 5, 30 ÷ 5 = 6, 5 x 6 = 30, 6 x 5 = 30

Page 218:
1. (loudly), barked;
2. (everywhere), looked;
3. (faster), swims; 4. (slowly), walked; 5. (early), awoke;
6. (outside), play

Page 219: 1. 0:11; 2. 2:11; 3. 1:11; 4. 3:11; 5. 5:11; 6. yellow

Page 220: 1. A; 2. Articles in newspapers or newsreels in movie theaters; 3. Because of him, we still rely on reporters in other countries for news and information as it is happening.

Page 221: 1. 30 students; 2. 95 students in 3rd grade, 105 students in 4th grade; 3. math; 4. 20 more students in 3rd grade; 30 more students in 4th grade

Page 222: Answers will vary.

Page 223: 1. 250 boxes; 2. 4 and 7; 3. 20 more boxes; 4. 10 fewer boxes; 5. 0, answers will vary.

Page 224: 1. My family visits Spring Grove, Minnesota, every year in the summer; 2. Dear Grandpa,; 3. Yours truly,; 4. On October 9, 2009, Carolyn saw the play; 5. My aunt and uncle live in North Branch, New York; 6. Dear Jon,; 7. January 1, 2010; 8. Paris, Texas, is located in the northeastern part of the state.

Page 225: 1. 6; 2. 6; 3. 7; 4. 9, 5. 4; 6. 8; 7. 6; 8. 4; 9. 5

Page 226: 1–2. Answers will vary.

Page 227: 1. well; 2. well; 3. better; 4. better; 5. best; 6. well; 7. worse

Page 228: 1. 32 cups; 2. $3,600; 3. 20 pounds; 4. 435 containers

Page 229: No answer required.

Page 230: 1. noun–berries, adjective–These, verb–smash, adverb–easily; 2. noun–soldiers, adjective–Ten, verb–march, adverb–together; 3. noun–pillow, adjective–big, verb–belongs, adverb–here

Page 231: 1. a place where people live together; 2. a city area where buildings are close together; 3. a country area where there is a lot of space between houses

Page 232: Line 1. heading; Line 2. greeting; Line 3. body; Line 4. closing; Line 5. signature

Page 233: 1. B; 2. It took up 1,800 square feet and weighed 50 tons; 3. 1947 to 1955; 4. Computers today are smaller, lighter, faster, less expensive, and can be operated by one person at a time.

Page 234: 1. 6, 6; 2. 3, 3; 3. 8, 8; 4. 4, 4; 5. 4, 4; 6. 4, 4

Page 235: Answers will vary.

Page 236:
1. The cold weather, (caused frost to cover the windows);
2. The falling snowflakes, (made my cheeks wet and cold);
3. (Snow stuck to my mittens), because I had made a snowman; 4. (The snowman melted), from the heat of the sun; 5. I swam so long in the pool, (that I needed to put on more sunscreen); 6. (Cayce missed the bus), because she overslept; 7. Because Shay watched a scary movie on TV, (she could not fall asleep); 8. The lady was thirsty, (so she went to get a glass of water)

Page 237: 1. A; 2. D; 3. B; 4. B; 5. C. 6. C

Page 238: Students should write the 3 lines of sender text in upper

Answer Key (continued)

left corner; Students should write the 3 lines of receiver text in the bottom center of envelope.

Page 239: 1. I, her; 2. him; 3. me; 4. us; 5. We; 6. They, us; 7. They, them

Page 240: 1. B; 2. They are organized so it is easy to get from one point to another; 3. Philadelphia has wide streets that are easy to walk down, but London has a maze of narrow streets that are hard to move around safely.

Page 241: Students should write the 3 lines of sender text in upper left corner; Students should write the 3 lines of receiver text in the bottom center of envelope.

Page 242:

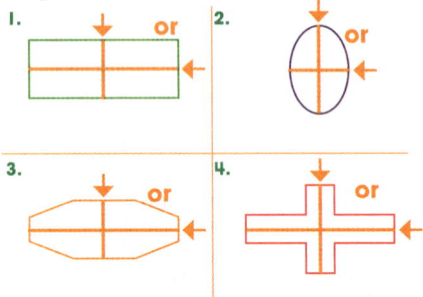

Page 243: 1. hard; 2. honk; 3. fingers; 4. round; 5. fly; 6. small; 7. pencil

Page 244: 1. Greg, Kipley, José, and Kira; 2. Day 1; 3. 2 lessons; 4. Naomi; 5. 5; 6. He is not a new student.

Page 245: Answers will vary.

Page 246: 1. no; 2. yes; 3. no; 4. yes; 5. no; 6. no

Page 247: 1. *Halloween Howl*; 2. Saturday; 3. yes; 4. Sunday; 5. Tuesday and Thursday

Page 248: 1. good; 2. better; 3. best; 4. bad; 5. worst; 6. good

Page 249: 1. C; 2. It has magnetic fields. 3. A magnetized needle inside a compass points toward Earth's magnetic north pole.

Page 250: 1. 1; 2. $1\frac{1}{2}$; 3. $\frac{1}{3}$; 4. $\frac{2}{3}$; 5. 1; 6. 1; 7. 1; 8. $1\frac{2}{5}$; 9. $\frac{3}{5}$

Page 251: 1–5. Answers will vary.

Page 252: 1. $14.00; 2. 3 oranges; 3. 344 pictures; 4. 407 books

Page 253: 1. B; 2. A; 3. A

Page 254: Answers will vary.

Page 255: 1. $3.39; 2. $6.41; 3. $2.89; 4. $1.06; 5. $2.89; 6. $6.28; 7. $2.09; 8. $2.11; 9. $3.89

Page 256: 1. A; 2. by sucking blood from another animal; 3. inside the body of an animal; 4. mistletoe and some types of ferns

Page 257: Answers will vary.

Page 258: 1. 8; 2. 12

Page 259: 1. F; 2. O; 3. F; 4. F; 5. O

Page 260: Answers will vary.

Page 261: 1. 140; 2. 10; 3. 20; 4. 43; 5. 165; 6. 40

Page 262: 1. B; 2–4. Answers will vary. 5. Solid–ice, liquid–water, gas–steam or vapor

Page 263: 1. 1; 2. 1; 3. $\frac{5}{7}$; 4. 1; 5. $\frac{2}{7}$; 6. $\frac{5}{6}$; 7. 1; 8. 1; 9. $\frac{2}{3}$

Page 264: 1. I; 2. ewe; 3. eye; 4. where; 5. you; 6. wear

Page 265: 1. O; 2. O; 3. O; 4. O; 5. F; 6. F; 7. F; 8. O; 9. F

Page 266: 1. C; 2. You will have a better chance of being a healthy adult later; 3. In your P.E. class and also outside of school; 4. Your family can go for a walk together.

Page 267: 1. H; 2. B; 3. A; 4. C; 5. E; 6. G; 7. D; 8. F; 9. J; 10. L; 11. I; 12. N; 13. O; 14. M; 15. K; 16. P

Page 268: Students should circle the following words: ninth, street, hillside, maine, march, skateboards, more, rock, avenue, detroit, michigan, whom, may, concern, it, please, sincerely, wesley, diaz

Page 269: 1. congruent; 2. congruent; 3. congruent; 4. not congruent

Page 270: 1. Raven has a new backpack. It is green and has many zippers. 2. Katie borrowed my pencil. She plans to draw a map. 3. Zoe is outside. She is on the swings. 4. Zack is helping Dad. Elroy is helping Dad too.

Page 271: 1. 10 gallons; 2. 1 liter; 3. 20 kilograms; 4. 7 ounces; 5. 11 inches; 6. 7 centimeters

Answer Key (continued)

Page 272: 1. any; 2. ever; 3. anybody; 4. anything; 5. have; 6. any; 7. anything; 8. anybody

Page 273: Answers will vary but may include: 1. outside in a forest or park; 2. summer; 3. wind blowing, creek bubbling, hawk screeching; 4. Answers will vary.

Page 274: Answers and drawings will vary.

Page 275: 1. B; 2. shorter; 3. the main idea (Ann and her brother took swimming lessons), important details (they took a bus, they liked it), and the conclusion (they learned how to swim by the end of summer)

Page 276: 1. 324 apples; 2. 12 people; 3. $7.95; 4. 2,525 pennies

Page 277: 1. S; 2. F; 3. R; 4. F; 5. S

Page 278: 1. globe; 2. encyclopedia; 3. dictionary; 4. encyclopedia; 5. globe; 6. globe; 7. encyclopedia; 8. dictionary; 9. dictionary

Page 279: 1. A; 2. C; 3. words with hidden meaning; 4. because knowledge is precious and should not be given to everyone

Page 280: 1. As a bird of prey, the American kestrel eats insects, mice, lizards, and other birds; 2. Birds of prey, such as hawks, have hooked beaks and feet with claws; 3. Falcons are powerful fliers, and they can swoop from great heights; 4. The American kestrel, the smallest North American falcon, is only 8 inches (20.3 cm) long; 5. "Kim, let's look at this book about falcons."

Page 281: 1. A; 2. An adult should help you to make sure you are being safe; 3. You shouldn't worry because important things can be discovered by mistake.

Page 282: 1. 20; 2. 20; 3. 10; 4. 7; 5. 6; 6. 18; 7. 121; 8. 22; 9. 20; 10. 6; 11. 6; 12. 30; 13. 2; 14. 30; 15. 49; 16. 7

Page 283: Answers will vary.

Page 284: 1. about 29; 2. 13; 3. 7

Page 285: Answers will vary.

Page 286: 1. less likely; 2. more likely; 3. impossible; 4. certain

Page 287: Answers will vary but the story should take place in the desert.

Page 288: 1. A; 2. B; 3. A

Page 289: 1. A; 2. It has 13 red and white stripes with 50 white stars on a blue background; 3. Texas is called the Lone Star state because its flag has one large star on it.

Page 290: 1. 2; 2. 3; 3. 2; 4. 3; 5. 3; 6. 3; 7. 2; 8. 1; 9. 2; 10. 5; 11. 3; 12. 4; 13. 1; 14. 5; 15. 3; 16. 2; 17. 1; 18. 3

Page 291: Answers will vary.

Page 292: Answers will vary.

Page 293: Answers will vary but should include the warm jar and place.

Page 294: 1. dairy cattle; 2. dairy cattle; 3. crops; 4. Answers will vary.

Page 295: 1. A; 2. Probes are special spacecraft; 3. Probes can gather information about what other planets looks like, and their weather and soil.

Page 296: 1–5. Drawings will vary but students should follow the directions.

Page 297: Answers will vary.

Page 298: 1. western; 2. eastern; 3. eastern; 4. western; 5. eastern; 6. eastern

Page 299: 1. He has always enjoyed school. 2. People who are in the hospital like to receive flowers. 3. Carl likes many things.

Page 300: No answer required.

Summer Quest™
Summer Workbook Series

Congratulations!

This certifies that

_____
Name

has completed **Summer Quest™ Activities**.

_____
Parent's Signature

American Education Publishing™

$\frac{10}{1}\frac{}{10} \quad \frac{10}{2}\frac{}{20} \quad \frac{10}{3}\frac{}{30} \quad \frac{10}{4}\frac{}{40} \quad \frac{10}{5}\frac{}{50} \quad \frac{10}{6}\frac{}{60} \quad \frac{10}{7}\frac{}{70} \quad \frac{10}{8}\frac{}{80} \quad \frac{10}{9}\frac{}{90} \quad \frac{110}{10}\frac{}{1100}$

$10\overline{)10}^{\,1} \quad 10\overline{)20}^{\,2} \quad 10\overline{)30}^{\,3} \quad 10\overline{)40}^{\,4} \quad 10\overline{)50}^{\,5} \quad 10\overline{)60}^{\,6} \quad 10\overline{)70}^{\,7} \quad 10\overline{)80}^{\,8} \quad 10\overline{)90}^{\,9}$

$10\overline{)100}^{\,10} \qquad 10\overline{)110}^{\,11} = 10\,r\,10$